Praise for *This Fresh Existence: Heart* from Bhikkhuni Dhammananda

I look to Venerable Dhammananda and her great community...as a revolutionary force for good for the future of Buddhism in the world. Her story, her life, and her courage are an example to all of us of what it means to speak truth to power, to stand in integrity, and to manifest unconditional wisdom and compassion. – **Roshi Joan Halifax**, from the Foreword

A beautiful dialogue with a wonderful and wise teacher. Dhammananda is a courageous pioneer, a nun who embodies blessings and points us to our inner freedom and compassion. – **Jack Kornfield**, author of *A Path with Heart*

We welcome this biography of Venerable Dhammananda Mahatheri, written by her close student Cindy Rasicot, which covers the life and challenges of the first Thai bhikkhuni, formerly known as Dr Chatsumarn Kabilsingh. Included in this inspiring account are teachings by Venerable Dhammananda, showing her own clarity and depth of understanding.

There was no one more qualified in Thailand to have taken on this historic role of restoring the Fourfold Sangha, as originally envisioned by the Buddha. Nonetheless, it took immense courage and innate dignity to receive this higher ordination for nuns in the face of the extreme criticism and personal denunciation that it evoked.

In the following years, Venerable Dhammananda Mahatheri has trained generations of women in the monastic role and, despite ongoing opposition from high-level ecclesiastics, she has continued to inspire many women to go forth as bhikkhunis in the Theravada tradition. We rejoice in her achievement and are grateful to the author for writing this important book. – **Jetsunma Tenzin Palmo**, author of *The Heroic Heart*, founder of Dongyu Gatsal Ling Nunnery, co-president of the International Buddhist Confederation

As told by her devoted follower, Cindy Rasicot, Venerable Dhammananda's story is one of courage, patience, and most of all compassion. Tracing her journey from scholar and TV personality to one of the first ordained nuns in modern-day Thailand, Rasicot's account of Venerable Dhammananda's life paints an inspiring picture of the woman responsible for reviving the bhikkhuni order in Thailand. – **Sharon Salzberg**, author of *Lovingkindness* and *Real Life*

Cindy has written an engaging and informative book about her beloved teacher Venerable Dhammananda, who through personal example has opened a viable pathway for Thai women to ordain as bhikkhunis in the Theravada tradition. We get a window into the considered thought, determination, and courage behind Venerable Dhammananda's decision to take ordination in 2003, and her tireless efforts since then to support and train other Thai women to do similarly. Prior to ordination as a bhikkhuni, she took the Bodhisattva Vow, which perfumes her whole approach. In the chapters exploring topics such as anger, patience, forgiveness, despair, and loneliness, which draw on dialogues between Venerable Dhammananda and those who are turning to her for guidance, her honesty, accessibility, kindness, and empathy come across, as well as her forthrightness. She teaches by way of illustration and shares her own working grounds. A strong faith in Sangha having the capacity to become an effective force for good in the world informs her approach, which emphasizes collective practice and altruistic activity. It is very good that through the pages of Cindy's book more people will learn of Venerable Dhammananda's life and work. – **Dharmacharini Anagarika Sanghadevi**, co-founder Taraloka Buddhist Retreat Centre for Women, author of *Living Together*

Cindy Rasicot's relationship with Bhikkhuni Dhammananda provides us with a precious opportunity to hear about Bhikkhuni Dhammananda's extraordinary life, her teachings, and some of the challenges she faced as she helped pave the road for Theravada Buddhist women to ordain. Rasicot's writing is elegant, sincere, profoundly inviting. With this book, we catch a glimpse of a remarkable teacher. What a wonderful contribution! – **Vanessa Sasson**, author of *Yasodhara and the Buddha* and *The Gathering: A Story of the First Buddhist Women*

The stories and perspectives of Buddhist women have long been overlooked and underrepresented. In *This Fresh Existence*, Cindy Rasicot shares her relationship with Venerable Dhammananda, Thailand's first fully ordained Theravada Buddhist Bhikkhuni. The book recounts the story of Venerable Dhammananda's life, shares her wise, compassionate teachings, and illuminates the struggle and controversy over women's full ordination for Theravada nuns that continues to this day. This is a story of great heart. In a world rife with divisiveness and pain, this intimate account of Venerable Dhammananda's courage, tenacity, and tenderness offers a potent balm. – **Pamela Weiss**, author of *A Bigger Sky: Awakening a Fierce Feminine Buddhism*

Heart Teachings
from Bhikkhuni Dhammananda

THIS FRESH EXISTENCE

Cindy Rasicot

ⓦ

Windhorse Publications
38 Newmarket Road
Cambridge CB5 8DT
info@windhorsepublications.com
windhorsepublications.com

Cover design by Katarzyna Manecka
Typesetting and layout Tarajyoti

British Library Cataloguing in Publication Data:
A catalogue record for this book is available from the British Library.

ISBN 978-1-915342-31-7

**A portion of the author royalties from the sale of this book will help
fund Venerable Dhammananda's Songdhammakalyani Temple in
Thailand.**

Dedication

This book is dedicated to Venerable Dhammananda.
Thank you Luang Mae, Venerable Mother.

Publisher's Acknowledgements

We would like to thank the Patrons who gave generously and anonymously to support the production of this book. One group donated in memory of Mallika, a great friend and teacher to many women in the Triratna Buddhist Order. Thank you.

And we also thank the individuals who donated through our 'Sponsor-a-book' campaign. You can find out more about it at https://www.windhorsepublications.com/sponsor-a-book/

Windhorse Publications wish to gratefully acknowledge a grant from the Future Dharma Fund and the Triratna European Chairs' Assembly Fund towards the production of this book.

Foreword

Historically, the *Theri*, or senior nuns, have been a mystery to most Buddhists. They stand like a distant mountain range covered in mist, not visible yet firmly there. It is only in recent years that more is being learned about the women who joined the Buddha's sangha (or community) two millennia ago. Their presence in early Buddhism created a quiet revolution in social values which only now is beginning to come to fruition in our modern cultures, thanks to the vision, courage, and determination of women like Venerable Dhammananda Bhikkhuni.

As Buddhism meets the modern world, more and more women are practising and being ordained as novices and fully ordained nuns. So also are women taking tremendous responsibility as the heads of monasteries, as dharma teachers, and as scholars. This book is about one of those extraordinary women, and I have the great joy of being her friend.

In 2002, I was fortunate to meet the great modern bhikkhuni Dr Chatsumarn Kabilsingh (now known as Venerable Dhammananda), a scholar of the Bhikkhuni Patimokkha – the monastic code for Theravada nuns. Dr Kabilsingh, a mother and a PhD, received full bhikkhuni vows in Sri Lanka on 28 February 2003, in the Theravada lineage – the first Thai woman to receive full bhikkhuni ordination.

Being a Buddhist feminist and social activist as well, I had wanted to meet this remarkable woman, spend time with and learn from her, and I got my chance at a meeting for monastics involved in socially engaged Buddhism. I was immediately moved by Venerable Dhammananda's presence. She spoke with profound conviction about the importance of allowing women to become fully ordained. I learned from some of the Thai monks who were present that there was not universal approval for her ordination, nor for the idea of ordaining women in general. Thailand has some 300,000 male monks, and the monk body has been a male monopoly for centuries. Women are essentially barred from ordination.

There is a fairly recent and unfortunate history associated with the lack of gender parity in the modern Thai monastic population. In 1928, Venerable Prince Jinavorn Siriwat, the Supreme Patriarch of Thailand, forbade male monks from ordaining women after Narin Klueng, a Buddhist activist and politician, had his two daughters ordained. For almost eighty years, this directive blocked women from joining the monk body. To make matters worse, in 1984 and 1987, the Sangha Supreme Council issued two rulings making the ordination of women illegal. So, this extraordinary act on the part of Dr Kabilsingh to seek full ordination, which had stirred up a powerful controversy in Thailand, was of great interest to me.

After the meeting, I made my way to her monastery, Wat Songdhammakalyani, 56 kilometres west of Bangkok in the city of Nakhon Pathom. I was shocked to witness the public hostility she was exposed to as a result of her ordination. The anger directed at her for realizing monastic vows was both bewildering and frightening.

While at Wat Songdhammakalyani, Venerable Dhammananda and I discovered we had much in common. We took refuge in each other, as I was weary from many problems in my country and community, and she was weary from the aggressive resistance to her ordination. We realized we both felt quite isolated and had few peers accessible to us. In our days together, we gave each other great support as we explored ways in which we could renew ourselves and continue our work in and for the world.

During this visit I learned from my new friend it was not a normal practice for a woman to do alms round in Thailand. Only male monastics engaged in this practice of walking silently holding an alms bowl and receiving food from laypeople as an expression of respect. Despite this taboo, Venerable Dhammananda invited me to join her in her daily alms round. She wore her russet Theravada robes and I my black Zen robes, and barefoot we made our way through the neighbourhood adjacent to the monastery. Each day I followed my friend down the rough roads. As we slowly walked in the heat of an early Thai morning, some households closed their doors tightly as we came near. Others opened their doors, and both men and women brought us food. Although my gaze was downcast, I was aware that some of the women wept as they stood before us. I saw men's hands shake as they put rice into our begging bowls.

At the time, I had no idea how radical an act this was. I only knew my head was bare to the sun, my feet were bare to the road, and my heart was bare as I received food from these generous laypeople. There are no photographs of these hot morning walks on the stinging pavement of Nakhon Pathom, but I had the sense the rights of women to practise as they saw fit were being established in some humble way as we made our way through this busy neighbourhood. Later, I realized we had not only broken the conventional practice, but we had, in some small way, broken open the door separating women practitioners from being who they really are in their country.

As I began to learn more about the situation concerning the rights of women in the Buddhist community in Thailand as well as other parts of Asia, Venerable and I began to discuss the icons of Buddhism that reflected values related to gender parity. I realized there were few images of women, especially in Southeast Asia. For example, I knew of no statues of Mahapajapati, the Buddha's stepmother who bravely became the first nun.

I learned from my friend that in fact there was a small temple called Wat Ratchanatdaram in the middle of Bangkok where there was a collection of statues of the first nuns. Venerable Dhammananda had never visited the temple, and we decided to do so together. Arriving at Wat Ratchanatdaram we found a guard who opened this sanctuary for us. King Rama III had built this little temple for his daughter on the occasion of his birthday. On entering the temple, we stood in front of the most wondrous sight of fifty-three Theris, each uniquely cast. At the head of this retinue of diverse beauty was a larger statue of Mahapajapati. This was an overwhelming and beautiful sight for Venerable Dhammananda and I, one that moved us to tears.

Since the mid-1960s, I have practised Buddhism. From my point of view, Buddhism is more of a philosophy and also a method to train the mind and heart. If we examine Buddhism's basic tenets we see that at its heart there should be no gender bias, but in fact there is. To this day, female Theravada monastics observing the Bhikkhuni Patimokkha are subject to eight precepts that favour their brother monks, precepts implying nuns are less worthy than the opposite sex. These are called 'the eight heavy rules' and were reputedly crafted by the Buddha, who resisted ordaining women until he was persuaded by his cousin Ananda, and influenced by the presence of his stepmother and her women associates. These rules were created some 2,500 years ago, and although faithfully observed by women monastics for centuries, are now being examined in the light of the twenty-first century, with the intent to honour the equal rights and capacity for awakening of both men and women.

Although it has not been typical for women to have positions of authority within traditional Buddhism, we now see a dramatic and positive change for women in all Buddhist orders. Buddhists like Venerable Dhammananda are setting policies in place to guarantee practitioners ethical treatment, honour families, and ensure democratic processes in their organizations, as they express their dedication to environmental justice and social engagement.

This means Buddhism is not only good for women, but good for the world. Much of this transformation has come about because of women like Venerable Dhammananda who, empowered as nuns and teachers, have empowered more and more women to do the same.

That women are receiving transmission and being ordained as monastics in our era is an extraordinary shift away from a patriarchal religion towards one honouring gender parity and practising what it preaches about inclusivity. This bodes well for Buddhism and all religions, as women like Venerable Dhammananda have so much to contribute to the psycho-social body of various religions, as well as the philosophy, ethics, and practices that ground religious institutions.

I believe we are experiencing a powerful phase shift in world religions today, led by women like Venerable Dhammananda, where gender parity is being deeply acknowledged and valued. The empowerment of women, the protection of children, the cultivation of ethics-based organizations, and the rights of all species is a vision whose time has come, although the women carrying this vision into the future are still deeply imperilled. I look to Venerable Dhammananda and her great community of novices and nuns as a revolutionary force for good for the future of Buddhism in the world. Her story, her life, and her courage are an example to all of us of what it means to speak truth to power, to stand in integrity, and to manifest unconditional wisdom and compassion.

Roshi Joan Halifax
Upaya Zen Center, Santa Fe, New Mexico
March 2023

A Healing Presence

I did not move to Thailand looking for a spiritual teacher, it simply happened. In August of 2005, my husband, thirteen-year-old son, and I relocated from our suburban home in northern California to Bangkok for my husband's job. Even though I was fifty-four years old when I met Venerable Dhammananda, I was not yet my own person. I did not have agency, direction, or backbone. Although excited to be living in Thailand, I was not particularly happy. I was in survival mode. A wife and mother first and foremost, I did not question my marriage of twenty years, and was not passionate about my career working for non-profit organizations. To the outside observer, I was a successful ex-pat mom, living a life of privilege in Bangkok, and while that was true, I was suffering from a deep sense of insecurity, as if I were missing an essential part of myself. I wanted to feel passionate about life, confident, and connected.

Perhaps that is why, soon after we arrived, I signed up for a conference sponsored by the Association of Women's Rights in Development and attended an afternoon workshop titled 'Faith, Feminism, and the Power of Love'. That is where I first encountered Venerable Dhammananda, Thailand's first fully ordained Theravada Buddhist nun. She was a tall, slender Thai woman dressed in saffron robes and flip-flops. Her head was a fuzzy crown of black shaven hair, and she wore thin gold wire-rimmed glasses. She possessed a quiet confidence as she spoke, and I still recall her words: 'We cannot solve anything with anger. Anger does not lead us anywhere. It is much harder to practice loving-kindness and compassion. That is the goal of Buddhism.'[1]

I felt chills as if she were speaking directly to me. I had struggled with anger all my life and intuitively knew I was blocked somehow, stuck in a negative cycle of resentment, sadness, and fear. I had never encountered anyone, particularly a Buddhist woman and a feminist, who spoke so quietly and radiated such a soft light. Her kindness was contagious, and I believe what drew me to her was my absolute faith in the power of her love.

At the end of the workshop, she invited anyone who was interested to visit her at Wat Songdhammakalyani, her temple in Nakhon Pathom. The following weekend I drove to the temple and during the three years I lived in Thailand spent a lot more time there, attending Buddhist ceremonies, and going on alms rounds to collect donations of food from local residents. I also had many one-on-one conversations with Venerable Dhammananda on topics as varied as *anatta* – no self – and the practice of compassion and forgiveness.

In the years since I first met Venerable Dhammananda, I have learned that being in her healing presence is a gift. There is something intensely compelling yet comforting about every word she speaks. When we talk, she gives me her full attention. Such is the power of her awareness; she is completely anchored in the here and now. While we are together the outside world drops away. There is no 'Cindy', there is no 'Venerable Dhammananda', there is only our connection. As she put it,

'Not being Cindy, not being *will*, just be.' When we experience being, we are one. We leave aside individuality and separation. Venerable Dhammananda says, 'To be anchored in the present is a mental exercise.' She makes this look deceptively easy, but the truth is, it takes years of mental training and meditation practice to be fully present.

When I sit with her, she transmits to me, as if by osmosis, her personal teachings. It is an energetic exchange, one which I sense with my whole being, like warm sunlight streaming in, and one I hope to share in these pages.

The story of how this book came to be written is worth telling. In 2008 I asked Venerable Dhammananda for permission to write about her life, and she graciously agreed. Almost as soon as we began, my husband received the news that he was being transferred back to the United States and we moved home. Because of the distance involved, we decided not to continue the project.

Venerable Dhammananda resurrected the book idea nine years later. I remember the day well. I was visiting the temple and having a hard time – discouraged about the state of my marriage. I wanted to speak to Venerable about my troubles. It was mid-afternoon, about two o'clock – the time when she regularly worked at her computer in her upstairs office. I debated whether to bother her because it was unusual to go in unannounced, but I was desperate.

I peered into the doorway and asked if we could talk. She smiled and motioned for me to come in. Before I could open my mouth to speak, I began to cry. I told her how lonely I felt, and she suggested, 'Remember when you said you wanted to write a book about me? I would like you to do that.' She gave me these simple instructions: 'Write about me the way you see me through your eyes.'

Later, she explained why she asked me to write the book. It was, in part, because she had similar feelings during the midlife crisis she experienced in 1981 when she was seriously depressed. During this time, she began to sketch simple line drawings. Alongside the sketches, she wrote about what the drawings meant. The book was eventually published and became a bestseller in Thailand. More importantly, she shared with me how working on the project over a period of about six months helped her recover from her depression. Venerable Dhammananda suggested I write a book because it would be a good way to cope with my problems while I took the time to heal. There were, of course, other reasons she asked me to write a book about her – she knew me well and trusted me – but that was how it happened.

After our conversation, I knew this would be my soul's work. Fast forward two years later, during another temple visit, I felt spiritually 'called' to write the book. At her previous evening's dharma talk, Venerable Dhammananda shared a Buddhist story about clinging and attachment. The following afternoon we met to talk, and she began by saying, 'Last night I told the story purposefully for you.'

I nodded. What happened next is hard to describe. I felt a tingling sensation around my head that permeated me completely, like a soft light filtering down to my heart. In a moment of complete consciousness, I felt her transmission and sensed an intuitive voice from deep inside telling me I would be a catalyst for her teachings, spreading her message of love and compassion throughout the world.

And so, I have written this book for two reasons: to tell the remarkable story of Bhikkhuni Dhammananda and to share her gentle wisdom and insights about how to live a more compassionate life. More than a biography or spiritual self-help book, I have endeavoured to illustrate the relationship – that elusive bond of love – that connects an unlikely student like me, a Western woman, together with a senior Asian Buddhist teacher.

The book is organized in three sections. Part I tells the story of Venerable Dhammananda's life, her personal struggles, her many professional accomplishments, and the challenges she faced in becoming the first fully ordained Thai woman in the Theravada tradition. Part II shares her wise teachings on topics like practising forgiveness, generating compassion, and coping with uncertainty. These teachings were gathered through personal conversations with her, and from selected dharma talks online. Venerable Dhammananda's instruction is simple and straightforward. She is a mother, grandmother, and great-grandmother, who was an influential and successful woman prior to being ordained at the age of fifty-seven. Because she has lived such a worldly life for so many years, she has a gift for making complex Buddhist teachings accessible to everyone through her use of clear language and personal examples. Part III, the last section of the book, takes a deeper look at the role and significance of ordination for women in Theravada Buddhism. I examine my own personal experience, having received temporary novice ordination twice, and offer Venerable Dhammananda's reflections on having been ordained for the past twenty years.

The History and Process of Female Ordination in Thailand

I learned about the history and process of female ordination in Thailand from Venerable Dhammananda because she has studied and written about it extensively, both as an academic for twenty-seven years and as a monastic. For a variety of reasons which are too detailed to explain here, Thailand never established a lineage of female monastics in its 700-year history prior to Venerable Dhammananda's ordination

Before proceeding further, I would like to provide some context about various types of ordination in Buddhism. As Buddhism spread out of India to Southeast Asia, East Asia, and now in the West and beyond, many forms of ordination have developed. For example, there are married priests in Zen and Pure Land Buddhism; there are Yogis in Tibetan Buddhism who can be either married or celibate, and in the Triratna Buddhist Order, for example, men and women receive ordination which is neither lay nor monastic; they live a committed religious life by following the dharma and working for the sangha, but without following traditional monastic rules.

Venerable Dhammananda was ordained in the Theravada tradition. Theravada Buddhism is considered the most orthodox branch of Buddhism and, as such, is committed to the rules for ordination set out in the texts of early Buddhism. I would like to introduce readers to women's ordination within the Theravada tradition since I refer to this process often throughout the book.

A woman goes through several steps before she is fully ordained. The first step is the lower novice or *samaneri* ordination during which she takes on ten precepts. Any novice who then wishes to seek higher ordination must complete a two-year training period as a *sikkhamana* (probationer) with a senior teacher. Without this training a woman cannot be considered a candidate for full ordination.

According to the eminent scholar of early Buddhism, Bhikkhu Analayo,

> When the Buddha ordained women, he did so on the condition that they accept the Eight Garudhammas also known as the eight principles to be respected. The sixth *garudhamma* states that a female candidate for higher ordination must observe a two-year training period as a probationer, a *sikkhamana*. After having observed this period of training, higher ordination should be requested by her from both communities, that is from the communities of *bhikkhus* (fully ordained Buddhist monks) and *bhikkhunis* (fully ordained Buddhist nuns).[2]

The ceremony for higher ordination is known as *upasampada* (full ordination). At this level, the woman becomes a bhikkhuni (fully ordained Buddhist nun). Venerable Dhammananda's novice and higher ordinations took place in Sri Lanka on 6 February 2001 and 28 February 2003, respectively. She had to travel to Sri Lanka to be ordained because Thailand does not permit monks to ordain women.

Even though there were no bhikkhunis in Thailand prior to Venerable Dhammananda, there was a form of religious life for Thai women known as *mae chi*. 'A mae chi is a woman, a lay renunciant, who shaves her head, wears a white robe, and observes either five or eight precepts.'[3] Essentially, these women adopt a monastic way of life without formal ordination. For the most part, mae chi are marginalized women in Thai society, uneducated, and without the financial support, considerable respect, and prestige usually granted to male monastics. They live in temples where they cook and clean for the monks but are not allowed to study the dharma.

The issue of women's ordination is controversial within the context of Thai Theravada Buddhism. Even though the Buddha ordained women in his lifetime, and some prominent senior bhikkhus support women's ordination, there is still significant opposition to female ordination. This statement by American scholar and Theravada monk Bhikkhu Bodhi sums up the controversy: 'If the Asian countries following Theravada Buddhism are to fully step into the modern world, it is clear they must explicitly permit women to receive full ordination, and that ordination has to be endorsed and upheld by the Sangha elders.'[4] The word 'sangha' is a Sanskrit and Pali word that means community. In this quote, Bhikkhu Bodhi is referring to the conservative opposition that exists within the current leadership hierarchy of the all-male Thai monastic sangha.

Near the end of his life, the Buddha spoke about the importance of the fourfold sangha, also known as the fourfold assembly, which consists of: bhikkhus (fully ordained Buddhist monks) and bhikkhunis (fully ordained Buddhist nuns), laymen and laywomen:

> In the *Mahaparinibbana Sutta*, which chronicles the
> Buddha's last days, the Buddha says he cannot pass away
> until he has 'accomplished, trained and skilled' disciples
> from all four categories of bhikkhus, bhikkhunis, laymen

and laywomen. Such disciples, according to the Buddha's own definition, would be able to expound the dharma, preach it, reveal it, and clarify it. In the story, it's concluded that he's succeeded, and so he is able to pass away.[5]

According to Bhikkhu Analayo, the Buddha 'intended from the outset to have bhikkhunis among his disciples. In other words, the granting of the going forth and higher ordination to female aspirants was an integral dimension of the Buddha's mission from its beginning.'[6] In taking this step, Venerable Dhammananda says, the Buddha uplifted women and placed them on a par with men.

An internationally recognized Buddhist scholar, Venerable Dhammananda spent years researching the original texts to confirm that the Buddha ordained women in his own time. I have often heard her say: 'The Buddha was the first feminist because he was the first religious leader in the world to acknowledge that women and men are equal spiritually. When the Buddha gave permission for women to be ordained in his lifetime, he declared that women can be enlightened. There is no other religion before Buddhism which so clearly recognized the spiritual potential of women.'

The Buddha not only elevated the status of women by recognizing them as capable of enlightenment, but he also confirmed their participation as ordained members of the fourfold sangha. Venerable Dhammananda explains the situation this way: 'You could say in my country that one leg of the chair – the fully ordained nuns – was missing. I needed to bring back this fourth leg.' Venerable Dhammananda has dedicated her life to restoring to women their rightful place in Buddhism.

Venerable Dhammananda has always emphasized the importance of the bhikkhuni sangha over the individual. It is not enough for a woman to ordain and then lead a solitary practice. She has said that an individual bhikkhuni, regardless of how admirable her practice is, will eventually pass away. A thriving sangha ensures that Buddhism will survive through the ages.

One last topic that needs clarification is temporary ordination. In Thailand almost all Buddhist men are temporarily ordained as novices. They enter the monkhood for a few months, often as young adults. This is seen as part of the son's duty to his parents, a way to honour them and give them religious merit. The ordination is often an elaborate, once-in-a-lifetime celebration.

Although it is a familiar practice for men, temporary novice ordination is a relatively new practice for women. Venerable Dhammananda wanted to give women the same opportunities as men. She felt that it was important for women, especially professionals with a college degree, to understand that they can be ordained as novices just like men. At her temple, temporary ordination is offered twice a year, on 6 April and 5 December, and it provides women with a chance to experience the monastic lifestyle. The opportunity is open to Thai and non-Thai citizens alike. During the novice ordination women come to live at the temple for nine days, take the ten precepts, study the spiritual teachings of Buddhism, shave their heads, wear the robes, and practise meditation in hopes of improving their overall peace and contentment once they return to their normal lives.

Venerable Dhammananda offers temporary novice ordination to women so they can gain a sense of appreciation for the beauty of the monastic experience. In some cases, women decide to become committed monastics. Since the programme's inception in 2008, nearly a thousand women have been ordained as samaneris (novices) in thirty-two ceremonies.

*

Venerable Dhammananda is a powerful role model particularly for women seeking to make positive changes in their lives. I once heard Venerable Dhammananda speak to a group of women volunteers at the National Museum of Bangkok. Someone in the audience asked if her decision to be ordained was difficult. 'No', she replied. 'I always chose my own path. When I set out to do something, I commit to it one hundred percent. I have a nickname – Stone – because I possess a rock like determination. I tell women who feel trapped by their circumstances to be courageous. My message is: number one, the way out is possible; number two, take the first step; number three, start now because everyone else is waiting around for someone else to start, so nothing happens. You can do it!'[7]

Venerable Dhammananda is a moral and spiritual compass for our times. Her actions support her words – she changed the landscape of her native Thailand when she became the first woman to receive full ordination in the Theravada Buddhist tradition. She is one of only a handful of ordained, Buddhist, feminist religious leaders in the world and one of the most important Buddhist teachers alive today.

When we consider the tremendous popularity of Buddhism in the West, there are many books written by and about male monastics but so very few by women, and it is vitally important that Bhikkhuni Dhammananda's voice be heard. We all need strong female role models, women who stand up in the face of adversity by following the path of their heart with courage, integrity, and determination.

In the West, we are increasingly consumers of technology and material goods, but we are not fully educated in the values of the human heart. Venerable Dhammananda describes Buddhism in one word: heart. She says, 'Change comes from the heart, not the intellect.'

Venerable Dhammananda has helped me understand that we can only be truly happy when we open our hearts to others. In the time I have known her, I have discovered more joy and personal harmony in my life. I hope like me, you will be truly inspired by her remarkable strength and kindness. I have benefited greatly from her teachings, and, in writing this book, I want to share these benefits with you. (Unless otherwise cited, all quoted speech that appears in single quotation marks was gathered from conversations I had with Venerable Dhammananda between 2005 and 2008.)

PART I

Herstory: The Path to Ordination

In 2012 Venerable Dhammananda wrote a book called Herstory about the lives of the original thirteen women ordained by the Buddha known as the Arahat Theris or Enlightened Nuns. She described the book as 'the story of women told by women' as she drew inspiration from these elders who pioneered the path for women's enlightenment. In fact, she admired them so much that she created clay sculptures and displayed them in a place of honour on the second floor of the main sanctuary of her temple.

Dhammananda sculpted clay images of the thirteen Arahat Theris

I have titled this section 'Herstory' to describe Venerable Dhammananda's path to ordination, which, similar to that of the Arahat Theris, is an inspiration for women in modern times.

CHAPTER 1

The Rebel Monk

We are on the right side of history.

Venerable Dhammananda in a contemplative pose

I am not exactly sure when it happened, but it was most likely the summer of 2016 – a very hot day at Venerable Dhammananda's monastery in Nakhon Pathom. All the nuns and laywomen had gathered near the front wall of the temple for the afternoon work session. There was a mound of soil that Venerable Dhammananda had asked us to remove and transfer to the back garden area.

I was sweltering under the Thai sun and not in the mood to be shovelling earth from one place to another. The task seemed senseless. Women lifted hoes and pickaxes, chipping away at the mound, inching their way forward bit by bit, leaving chunks of semi-dry earth and rock. Several of us followed with shovels and plastic buckets to haul their debris away. We stood side by side in an assembly line, passing the buckets from hand to hand until they reached the last person, who dumped the contents into a large wheelbarrow.

The sweat dripped from my face as my resentment grew. *Why do I have to do this?* Just then, Venerable Dhammananda stepped forward, hoe in hand. She lifted the tool above her head and with a mighty blow brought it down, smashing the earth to pieces. I was stunned. She was remarkably strong for a person in her early seventies. For me, that single blow symbolized the strength of her determination.

The Rebel Monk

Venerable Dhammananda, previously known by her lay name, Dr Chatsumarn Kabilsingh, did not begin to think seriously about being ordained until her mid-fifties. At the time she had enjoyed a highly successful career as a professor of Buddhist studies for twenty-seven years at Thammasat University, was a well-known media personality who hosted a popular TV dharma show, and had been married for thirty years with three adult sons.

She claimed the 'DNA for ordained life' was 'in her blood' and is proud of her ancestors. Her maternal grandmother, Somcheen, was illiterate but in her later years was ordained as a mae chi and became leader of the temple women at Wat Khanikaphala in Bangkok. Before she died, Somcheen predicted she would be reborn one year from the date she passed away. Indeed, exactly one year later, on 6 October 1944, her granddaughter, Chatsumarn, was born.

Continuing the religious tradition her grandmother began, Venerable Dhammananda became the first fully ordained

Theravada nun in Thailand in 2003. She had to travel to Sri Lanka to do this because Thailand does not permit women to be ordained. At the time, Thailand had approximately 300,000 male monks and no ordained women, leading the Thai press to dub her the 'Rebel Monk'. She said, 'I never felt like a rebel. I simply did what the Buddha allowed me to do, which was to be ordained. I was waiting for others to ordain. In fact, I went to a few other women who I thought might be interested in joining me, but they were not, so I went ahead and did it alone.'

As mentioned previously, in the context of Thailand's history as a nation, the lineage of female monastics – samaneris (female novices) and bhikkhunis (fully ordained nuns) – never took hold. Venerable Dhammananda saw it as her responsibility to introduce this missing heritage that the Buddha had granted women. She knew from her academic studies that the history of the bhikkhuni sangha in Thailand occurred in three waves. The first attempt to establish a bhikkhuni order began in 1928, when Narin Phasit (1874–1950) arranged for his daughters Sara and Chongdi to be ordained. Originally, they were ordained as samaneris, but eventually Sara, the eldest, became a bhikkhuni. Narin had been a successful provincial governor early in his career but became disillusioned with the system. He was an embattled public figure, known for his outspoken criticism of the government and the Thais. His calls for political and religious reform landed him in jail several times. He spoke about the importance of establishing a bhikkhuni order for many years before his daughters' actual ordinations took place and wanted to restore the missing link in the Buddha's fourfold community of laymen, laywomen, bhikkhu, and bhikkhuni.

The exact details of where or how Narin's daughters were ordained – even which monks ordained them – were unclear because the event was done in secret. According to Narin's later account the ceremony took place in April of 1928. Following this, the sisters lived in Nonthaburi province along the banks of the Chao Phraya River at Narin's elaborate family compound. Part of the living arrangement was designated as a monastery for women, called Wat Nariwong. Venerable Dhammananda indicated there were 'six other nuns living alongside the two sisters at the monastery'.[8]

Narin's attempt to ordain his daughters was not successful. Two months after the ceremony was performed, the Supreme Patriarch (religious head of the Thai Buddhist sangha appointed by the King) issued a decree prohibiting monks from giving ordination to women. The decree, known as the 1928 Sangha Act, proclaimed that bhikkhunis must be present to ordain the women, otherwise ordination was not possible.

The nuns living in Narin's compound apparently remained in robes for more than a year despite the decree, but at some point they were spotted on their morning alms round. In September of 1929 government officials intervened, and all eight women were put on trial. During the hearing the women were told that by claiming to be ordained and putting on robes similar to those of monks, they had engaged in an act that 'disgraced the religion'.[9] They were asked to disrobe. Four of them complied, but Chongdi was among the nuns who refused. The convicted women 'fought off a group of prison guards and female inmates deployed to carry them off to prison'.[10] Eventually they were imprisoned and forced to disrobe.

Sara and Chongdi

The 1928 Sangha Act, often referred to as 'the bhikkhuni ban', is still cited by the Thai government in upholding the country's refusal to accept ordained women. In Thailand the Thai sangha is closely linked to the government. In *The Bhikkhuni Lineage*, a pamphlet Venerable Dhammananda wrote in 2004, she referred to the Sangha Act as the 'first structural violence against women, in black and white', because, essentially, it 'defined Sangha as only (being) a community of monks'.[11]

Venerable Dhammananda gained valuable insights from Narin's failed attempt. The fact that he conducted the ordination in secret was cited as a problem because no one knew if the required number of bhikkhus was present. There may have been only one bhikkhu present to give ordination, in which case it was not done properly in accordance with the Vinaya – the rules and procedures that govern the Theravada Buddhist sangha. By the time Venerable Dhammananda decided to receive full ordination, she knew it would have to be done in public, and with a minimum of five bhikkhus present.

The Second Wave

The second wave of Thailand's bhikkhuni lineage began with Venerable Dhammananda's own mother, Voramai Kabilsingh, in the mid-1950s. Following a tumour scare, Voramai became interested in Buddhist meditation and published a Buddhist magazine that continued for thirty-two years. On 2 May 1956, Voramai took her then eleven-year-old-daughter, Chatsumarn, and her three adopted children to a barbershop, where she promptly asked to have her head shaved. After the barbershop, they went to Wat Bovornives, where Voramai received vows from Phra Prommuni, her teacher and deputy abbot of the temple.

Voramai informed her teacher that she did not want to be a mae chi because she understood the limitations on women's monastic identity in Thai Buddhism and was determined to overcome them. She was inspired by the women who were ordained as bhikkhunis in the Buddha's time and 'believed that since the bhikkhuni sangha was established by the Buddha, any woman who wanted to be ordained should be regarded as a bhikkhuni. At one point she even went to Bodh Gaya, India, sat under the Bodhi tree where the Buddha became enlightened, and requested direct ordination from the Buddha. She then spent two weeks in meditation there.'[12]

Technically, Voramai was not 'ordained' as a samaneri (novice) that day in May of 1956. She received the eight precepts from her teacher, which meant she had the same status as a mae chi. However, according to Venerable Dhammananda, 'My mother proclaimed herself *nakbuad*, an ordained person, and wore a light-yellow robe to make it clear to everyone that she was not a mae chi.'

Venerable Voramai newly ordained wearing her light-yellow robe

Four years after her ordination Venerable Voramai founded Wat Songdhammakalyani Temple, the first temple in Thailand established by and for Buddhist women. She built a private school for children from kindergarten to sixth grade, which also functioned as an orphanage. She engaged in social welfare projects providing food and clothing for the poor. She was very committed to a life of social service. Venerable Dhammananda grew up in her mother's temple, raised her three sons there, and continues to reside there as Abbess today.

Not long after the temple was established, the Mayor of Nakhon Pathom became suspicious of Voramai's activities, and reported her to the Council of Elders, the governing body of the Buddhist sangha in Thailand, saying she was challenging their authority by wearing yellow robes. She was summoned before the Council.

Venerable Dhammananda wrote about her mother's case in *The Bhikkhuni Lineage*. 'The charge was 'impersonating the Bhikkhu'. Her teacher Phra Prommuni was a member of the Council of the Elders and defended her. He asked a logical question: could a monk ever wear a light-yellow robe? The monks answered no. Phra Prommuni asked the monks why, since the light-coloured robe could not be worn by the sangha, they were objecting to it. The Council of Elders made the determination that wearing the light-yellow robe was not causing any harm to the sangha.[13] This was the only time Voramai experienced open conflict with the government. After that, there were no more incidents of outside interference from the government or the Thai sangha.

Years later, during her postgraduate studies at McMasters University in Canada in 1971, Chatsumarn learned that bhikkhuni ordination was possible in Taiwan and encouraged her mother to travel there to receive full ordination as a bhikkhuni in the Mahayana or Chinese tradition, which she did. Her mother became the first modern Thai bhikkhuni and, in her case, because the ordination was Mahayana and not Theravada, the Thai sangha did not raise strong objections. 'To the general public in Thailand, Venerable Voramai is still only a *mae chi*. To the Thai Sangha, her status is that of a Mahayana Bhikkhuni, and she is not part of the Thai Theravada tradition.'[14]

Venerable Dhammananda learned several lessons from her mother's experience. She understood that ordination alone was not enough; it must be combined with training. Venerable Voramai's ordination was given in Chinese and since her mother did not speak or read the language, she could not appropriately study the Vinaya (monastic code of rules). Venerable Dhammananda believes that understanding the Vinaya is important, 'so that we can follow it properly and practise accordingly'.

Venerable Dhammananda recognized that 'the purpose of all our struggles from my mother's time to my time was to start a sangha. Buddhism is successful because of the sangha. If the Buddha was alone and no one followed in his footsteps, Buddhism would have died out 2,500 years ago.'

Although her mother had many loyal female followers, Venerable Voramai remained the lone bhikkhuni. There was no community of ordained women living with her. At the time, Thai society had very little knowledge about bhikkhunis or the possibility of ordination, so she was not able to start a sangha, yet Venerable Dhammananda was grateful to her mother for starting the temple and 'preparing the ground for us'.

The Third Wave

The third wave of bhikkhuni ordination in Thailand began with Venerable Dhammananda's samaneri (novice) and bhikkhuni (full) ordinations in 2001 and 2003, which happened more than seventy years after the first Thai woman's attempt to ordain. Venerable Dhammananda drew three important lessons from history: the ordination must be conducted properly, it must be done in public, and it had to be combined with sufficient training. She ensured that all three of these conditions were met when she received samaneri and bhikkhuni ordination.

Before she left for Sri Lanka in 2001 Venerable Dhammananda hired a photographer to document her ordination. 'I was clear that it must be recorded, because as soon as I returned to Thailand, I knew people would be asking me, how was it done?' There was a bhikkhuni preceptor present at her samaneri ordination, and the required number of bhikkhus and bhikkhunis present at both her samaneri and bhikkhuni ordinations as stipulated in the Vinaya.

Venerable Dhammananda followed the Vinaya and honoured her commitment to establish a bhikkhuni sangha in Thailand. She has been amazingly successful. Today there are more than 285 bhikkhunis (fully ordained nuns) in Thailand, spreading out in at least thirty of the country's seventy-seven provinces.

Venerable Dhammananda pictured with an earlier photo of her mother

We Are on the Right Side of History

Venerable Dhammananda's novice ordination in Sri Lanka instigated a huge public debate in the Thai media, which referred to it as the 'bhikkhuni debate' and the 'Dhammananda controversy'. The height of the controversy was from April 2001 to June 2001. Due to her celebrity status prior to ordination, people followed Venerable Dhammananda's story closely, and she was targeted by newspapers, radio talk shows, internet sites, magazines, books, and in public meetings. She faced a wave of vitriolic criticism by senior orthodox Thai monks. 'The first three months after my ordination I was attacked in the media and received nasty email messages. I did not read the newspapers for two years because the negative press was so strong.'

An article in the *Bangkok Post* entitled 'Her holiness' summarized the controversy:

> To a certain extent, Buddhist scholar Dr. Chatsumarn Kabilsingh had expected some resistance when she decided to be ordained as a Theravadin samaneri in Sri Lanka earlier this year. After all, Thailand has never had a bhikkhuni Sangha. Thai law prohibits monks from ordaining women as samaneri or bhikkhuni. The backlash from senior monks over Dr. Chatsumarn's ordination has been daunting.[15]

The commentary in the same article continued:

> A few senior monks have come out to voice dissent. [. . .] The bhikkhuni lineage in the Theravada tradition terminated a long time ago, some say. There is no need to further investigate or reinterpret existing rules to accommodate the demands of women who wish to live a religious life. End of conversation. 'The Bhikkhuni ordination requires dual ordination from both the bhikkhu and bhikkhuni sangha' [. . .] Since there is no bhikkhuni in Thailand ordination is simply impossible.[16]

The question of dual ordination, which had been raised seventy years earlier, resurfaced; however, this time the argument was more complicated because of an important event in Sri Lanka in 1998. Historically, both the male and female Theravada monastic orders thrived in Sri Lanka from the third to the eleventh century, but then died out when Islamic armies invaded the country. Over time, the male monastic order survived but the female lineage died out.

Venerable Dhammananda claimed that 1998 was a significant year for Theravada bhikkhunis because it was when the bhikkhuni lineage was reinstated in Sri Lanka. The international ceremony to revive the bhikkhuni sangha was held in Bodh Gaya, India – the most important of the Buddhist pilgrimage sites, the place where the Buddha attained enlightenment. Venerable Dhammananda was invited to attend the international ordination ceremony held by the Chinese organization Fo Guang Shan because at the time she was a professor known for her interest in the bhikkhuni Vinaya.

'The proceedings', Venerable Dhammananda said, 'were held at a Chinese, Mahayana temple. The Chinese bhikkhus and bhikkhunis ordained the twenty Sri Lankan *dasa sil mata* (a category similar to a mae chi) in the Mahayana tradition. Sri Lankan monks were present to witness the ceremony, but they did not officiate.'

The Sri Lankan monks faced a dilemma after the ordination in Bodh Gaya. They raised a legitimate question: could a woman ordained in the Mahayana tradition 'be recognized as valid from a Theravada legal viewpoint?'[17] Mahayana and Theravada are different schools of Buddhism, with different sets of monastic rules and practices. Theravada means 'way of the elders' and refers to the orthodox teachings of the Buddha in the fifth century BCE. Mahayana is referred to as the 'great vehicle' and originated in the first century CE. The Mahayana tradition is more flexible about the orthodoxy of the Buddha's original teachings and is prevalent in China, Tibet, Japan, and Korea, whereas Theravada Buddhism is prevalent in Sri Lanka, Thailand, Myanmar, Cambodia, and Laos.

The Sri Lankan monks devised a plan to thwart potential critics; they decided to take the Sri Lankan bhikkhunis ordained in Bodh Gaya back to Sarnath, Sri Lanka, to perform a second ordination, this time in the Theravada tradition. This second ceremony was called *dalhikamma* or confirmation. Once this happened, Venerable Dhammananda was convinced the Sri Lankan women were legally and fully ordained and could, therefore, ordain women from other Theravada countries. That is why she ultimately decided to be ordained in the Theravada tradition in Sri Lanka.

Thai monks disagreed with Venerable Dhammananda's interpretation and discounted the 1998 revival. Phra Dhammapitaka, the religious authority in Thai Theravada Buddhism at the time, said, 'It's like you graduated from a different university and then demand you are approved by another establishment. The clergy doesn't have any right to grant that kind of approval.'[18]

In May 2001, in the wake of the intensifying debate, the Supreme Patriarch, Somdet Phra Yanasangworn (head of the Thai Sangha), voiced his disapproval of the ordination, citing the 1928 decree in full which clearly stated that the bhikkhuni lineage had long been extinct. While delivering an address to students graduating from a Buddhist university, he warned them not to 'dare offend the Buddha with wrongful speech and action that defy his stipulation, (or they) would not live a good life' (reported in *Naewna* a Thai local newspaper).[19]

There were other disparaging comments like that of Phra Dhepdilok, deputy abbot of Wat Bovornives, who reportedly said, 'If we allow women to be ordained as bhikkhunis and to establish their own monasteries, they can be attacked, even raped. Such a thing will weaken Buddhism.'[20]

Some monks claimed she ordained for personal fame. Venerable Dhammananda disagreed and said, 'Critics claimed that I pursued ordination for personal gain. I did not choose to be ordained because I want people to recognize me. I did it because I want to carry on the heritage of the Lord Buddha, to revive the four pillars of Buddhism bhikkhus, bhikkhunis, laymen and laywomen – that will sustain the religion into the future. I don't mind if some people reserve different opinions about bhikkhunis. The public will be the ones to judge our worth.'[21]

Throughout the controversy and personal attacks, Venerable Dhammananda did not respond in anger or hatred; she faced the adversity with patience and determination. She said, 'I even challenged people who criticized me behind my back to come to the temple and speak to me directly, but they never did.'

I once asked her if she thought she was brave, but she denied it. 'Actually, I have no bravery. All I have is strong faith in the Buddha.' She explained her decision this way: 'I have traversed the globe so that my grandchildren will be proud of their grandmother who cleared the path for them to walk proudly as Buddhist women. We are on the right side of history.'

Venerable Dhammananda's 2003 ordination ceremony in Sri Lanka

On 28 February 2003, Venerable Dhammananda returned to Sri Lanka to receive the full bhikkhuni ordination referred to as *upasampada*. This time, there was little public discussion. Venerable Dhammananda said, 'The negativity people expressed before, kind of backfired on them because they spoke up about things they did not understand, and their comments were a matter of public record. Their allegations were false and could not be proven in the Tripitaka [the book of the Buddha's sacred scriptures].'

Following her ordination, Venerable Dhammananda was more determined than ever. 'Speaking at her temple within days of her return from her bhikkhuni ordination ceremony in Sri Lanka in 2003, Venerable Dhammananda was particularly earnest and optimistic. Ordained women, she said, 'must realize that we are in a very important situation, that whatever we do will greatly affect the existing movement'.[22]

'She also pointed to the advantages of social change that women of her time enjoyed compared to those of previous generations. In her view the process of globalization with its far-reaching media and information networks, the higher level of education of both ordained women and members of society in general, and her effort to "build up the structure to support the bhikkhuni sangha" – all contributed to the strength of the present movement.' 'With great spirit she declared, "We must succeed because we are the third wave. We have so much information from the first and second wave(s,) we cannot allow any further failure (*Yasodhara* 2003: 7)"'[23]

And she remained true to her conviction. In July of 2007, four years after her bhikkhuni ordination, Dhammananda attended the first International Congress on Buddhist Women's Role in the Sangha. The conference, convened by His Holiness the Dalai Lama, was held in Hamburg, Germany and aimed to create worldwide consensus on the need for establishing full ordination of bhikkhunis in the Tibetan tradition. At that time, some people hoped that His Holiness would issue a statement sanctioning bhikkhuni ordination.

On the last day of the conference His Holiness came before a hushed audience of 1,200 participants; women were in the majority. There were Chinese nuns from Taiwan wearing yellow and brown robes and Vietnamese nuns wearing mustard yellow ones. The bhikkhunis from the Theravada tradition wore various shades of brown and saffron robes. The Tibetan samaneris and bhikkhunis wore maroon robes.

A nine-member panel of monastics was seated on stage in front of the audience; His Holiness sat in the middle with bhikkhus to his right and bhikkhunis to his left. Dhammananda was on the end seat. All of the panellists supported higher ordination of women. Each panellist had three minutes to speak. After everyone had spoken, His Holiness pulled out a sheet of prepared remarks and stated, 'Since a Bhikshuni Sangha has long been established in the East Asian Buddhist traditions (of China, Taiwan, Vietnam, and Korea) and is presently being revived in the Theravada tradition of South Asia (especially Sri Lanka), the introduction of the Bhikshuni Sangha within the Tibetan Buddhist tradition should be considered seriously and favorably.'[24] However, he concluded by saying, 'But in terms of the modality of introducing Bhikshuni vows within the tradition, we have to remain within the boundaries set by the Vinaya – otherwise, we would have introduced the Bhikshuni vow in the Tibetan Buddhist tradition long time ago.'[25] In other words, if the Buddha were alive today, he undoubtedly would have supported bhikkhuni ordination, but since he was not, His Holiness could not make that decision on his behalf.

Dhammananda said she was crestfallen when she heard these words. She raised her hand and respectfully said, 'Your Holiness, when the Buddha was about to die, he did give permission that minor rules may be lifted if the Sangha should decide to go ahead. So, you don't need to wait for the future Buddha.'

The audience broke into applause.

CHAPTER 2

Healing the Mother–Daughter Relationship

If you want love from another person, ask yourself, have I given her love?

Cindy and Venerable Dhammananda at the temple in 2006

In July of 2006, almost nine months after my first encounter with Venerable Dhammananda, I wrote an article about her for an English-language Thai arts and culture magazine. I arranged to visit her temple and provided my driver with directions to Wat Songdhammakalyani, her monastery located about an hour's drive west of Bangkok in the city of Nakhon Pathom.

As we sped along Petkasem highway with its grey, soot-covered buildings, noisy trucks, and smell of diesel fuel, I looked for the landmark – a large Chinese Buddha at the entrance. He sits on a pedestal, full bellied, holding a thick strand of round beads in his hand.

The Chinese Buddha seated at the entrance to the temple

It was mid-morning when we drove past the Buddha and parked inside. The first thing I noticed was the quiet. Time slowed as my concerns faded and my awareness shifted to my current surroundings. I stopped to admire a life-size statue of

Quan Yin, the Bodhisattva of Compassion, sealed in a glass case. She looked radiant. Transfixed by her gaze I stood silent, immersed in a sea of serenity.

Quan Yin

I slowly turned away and walked past the *uposatha* hall (main temple) towards the front office. I delicately stepped over a black dog who was napping by the sliding glass door and slid it open. Inside, a heavyset nun wearing brown robes and wire-rimmed glasses looked up, waved me in, and asked for my passport. I told her about my appointment with Venerable

Dhammananda and she led me around the corner of the building to the dining area, a wide-open rectangular space with a wooden roof, two rows of ceiling fans, and long metal tables with blue plastic chairs.

Venerable Dhammananda rounded the corner and smiled. She sat down, patted the seat next to her, and began talking about an experience she had during her alms round. 'This morning I visited a woman who was in the last stage of cancer. She was too weak to come outside so I went indoors to her bedside and held her in my arms while I chanted the Medicine Buddha's blessing for her – reciting his full name and praising him as the Great Healer – with the intention of helping her cross over into enlightenment.'

'It was so moving', she said, lifting her hand to her heart.

Adjusting her robes, Venerable Dhammananda's face became pensive. She said, 'My mother was a great mystic and healer with a large following of supporters from all over the country. Her ordained name was Venerable Voramai, but everyone affectionately called her "Venerable Grandma", or *Luang Ya* in Thai. I am proud of my mother for building this temple more than fifty years ago.'

It struck me that fifty years ago Venerable Dhammananda could not have been more than a teenager. I tried to imagine what her life was like growing up in a temple and asked her how old she was when her mother was ordained.

'I was eleven. It was May 1956. My mother took me, her only biological child, and my three adopted siblings to the barbershop. We stood against the back wall and watched as my mother had her hair shaved off.' Venerable Dhammananda leaned into the table. 'It was very strange, but none of us spoke.

36

I guess we were all stunned. I was very self-conscious that people were staring at us because my mother was having her head shaved. It was so typical of her not to communicate with us. Afterwards we went to Wat Bovornives where my mother received the precepts from her teacher.'

I paused to consider what Venerable Dhammananda was saying. I wondered what it was like to be parented by such a determined woman and asked her what her relationship to her mother was like. 'Growing up with my mother was not easy. She was the lawgiver, with very high standards.' As a child Venerable Dhammananda never argued with her mother, she simply obeyed her and did what she was told. 'I never experienced the softness of a mother–daughter relationship. Once on my birthday I asked for a party and she said, "That is just sissy stuff."'

Venerable Dhammananda said she felt lonely, insecure, and anxious growing up. 'I tried to be perfect because my mother had such high expectations of me. I remember when I was about ten, when my mother received visitors, I would sit beside her and fan her to keep her cool. If my mouth fell open in front of the guests, she would pinch me. I would straighten up and sit properly like a lady. I was a bundle of nerves and suffered so much. I wanted her love and affection, but she could not give that to me.'

She looked dismayed. 'When I was three and a half, my mother sent me to live with her sister in Bangkok to start my formal education. This was about the time my parents separated. We had been living in the Southern Province of Trang. Being a teacher, my mother was concerned about the social setting in Trang, where there was a lot of gambling and crime. This was the first time I experienced *dukkha* [suffering].'

'My aunt did not have any children of her own. I was alone. She never touched me or took my hand. The hardest part of the day happened when I came home from school. I suffered being cut off from my family and felt a deep sense of loneliness that haunted me for years.' [26]

I was touched by what Venerable Dhammananda had shared. I could relate to her experiences of feeling lonely, anxious, and insecure growing up. There were so many similarities between our mothers. My mom, an attorney who graduated first in her law school class in the mid-1930s, was ahead of her time. Being practical and lawyerly, she did not dwell in the world of 'soft' emotions and feelings. I spent a lot of time alone as a child and yearned for her affection.

Like Venerable Dhammananda's mother, mine was often critical of me. In high school, we argued constantly; she would yell, I would grow defensive and respond in anger. The longer we argued, the worse I felt, and shame would overcome me, along with a sense that I was somehow to blame. Over time, I withdrew into myself, a stew of hurt and resentment bubbling below the surface. I was angry at myself, but also secretly blamed my mother because she was not able to love me the way I wanted. Unable to forgive my mother, I was incapable of loving myself.

I do not know how long I sat lost in my thoughts, but when I looked up, Venerable Dhammananda was petting one of the dogs that lived on the temple grounds. This dog was white with black spots and although its markings suggested a dalmatian, it was squat like an oversized dachshund. 'Your mother sounds so similar to mine', I said. Venerable Dhammananda glanced over at me. I couldn't help noticing the peaceful calm in her eyes and healing radiance about her. There was a softness in her voice as she said, 'In order to heal ourselves, we must heal the mother–daughter relationship.'

A feeling of sadness came over me. My eyes welled up with tears, and I began to cry. Venerable Dhammananda reached across the desk and gently touched my hand. I felt as if she could see straight through to my soul. 'It's okay', she said. 'People often cry when they first arrive. You build up a wall around yourself, and that wall starts to peel off, and you allow that soft "you" to come out. I believe change comes from the heart, not from the intellect. You must feel it. If you have to weep, then weep, and it opens you up and leads you to change.'[27]

She looked down for a few seconds, adjusted her sash over her left shoulder, and then said, 'Let me tell you a story… When I was in my early forties, still a layperson and a professor of Buddhist Studies at Thammasat University, I went to a conference and heard a woman whom I'll call "Mary" share an experience that had a profound impact on me and changed my relationship to my mother.

'Mary stood in front of the group talking about her father, who was very abusive. When he came home, he would beat his wife while Mary and her sister hid under the table. She hated her father. One day, he left home and never returned. Her mother struggled to support her daughters by cleaning homes. Mary received a good education, finished her PhD, and married a kind Indian man.

'Many years later, Mary's father returned out of the blue. He soon discovered he had cancer. He exclaimed, "Why me? I never harmed anyone in my life." Mary was taken aback because she remembered how abusive he was. Even though she carried these painful memories, she decided to take care of him. Over time, he became weaker and weaker and was like a skeleton.

'In his final days, he received morphine because his pain was so intense, but one day he asked the nurse not to give him any medication because he wanted to talk to his daughter. When Mary came in to visit, he could not speak, but she read his lips as he mouthed, "I love you." She was surprised. By this time, she was a Buddhist and a psychologist, and after his funeral, she decided to investigate his life. She found out he had an older brother who was killed in a car accident when he was six. The older boy had been his mother's favourite, and she said hurtful things like, "Why weren't you killed instead?" Once Mary understood this, she truly forgave her father because she realized he never received any love, so he did not know how to give love.'

Venerable Dhammananda dropped her gaze, 'By the time Mary finished telling her story, everyone was crying; there was not one dry eye in the room. I realized my mother had gone through something similar. When I looked back on her childhood, I realized my mother's parents did not show her any affection. She was the sixth daughter in a family of girls, and her father always wanted a son. Her father rejected her because she was not a boy.

'Many years later when I was an adult, I happened to read a diary entry she wrote in 1944 – the year I was born. Early in her pregnancy, she went to pay respect to the main temple in Nakhon Si Thammarat, a major province in the South, where she promised to give fifty gold leaves as an offering of thanks if she were to have a son.'

Venerable Dhammananda nodded her head in emphasis, 'That is how much she wanted a boy.'

'My mother always favoured my adopted brother', she said, sounding slightly irritated. 'While I was teaching and struggling to go to work, I spent long hours travelling on the bus to my job at the university. Even so, my mother bought my brother a new car for 400,000 *baht* [$11,000]. I was so hurt. I felt she loved my brother more than me, even though she literally picked him up off the street.'

Venerable Dhammananda tilted her head in a thoughtful manner. 'Soon after hearing Mary's story, I realized my mother's parents never praised her or showed her any physical affection. When you realize the person who has harmed you is also trapped in this cycle of suffering, it becomes possible to forgive them. Once I understood her situation, I started to hug her after I bowed to her. Even though she would say, "Don't do that", I could tell she enjoyed it. When I began to express physical affection, our relationship improved.

'I looked back at my childhood and realized that she *did* express love for me, but in her own way. She had a very hard life. I was so young when my mother and father separated, and she became a single parent. The whole time I was growing up, she struggled financially and had to worry about earning money to take care of me and my adopted sisters and brother. Four mouths, like four birds waiting to be fed. She did not have time to play with us.

'My desire to be loved was very self-centred. I had not stopped to consider her situation but, once I did, I really appreciated everything she had done for her children. This was an important lesson for me. I always remind people: you do not know what kind of life your mother or father had. We can heal our relationships to our parents by becoming more compassionate. If you want love from another person, ask yourself, have I given her love? When we start giving love, we receive it in return.'

Venerable Dhammananda and I sat together, absorbed in the silence. As our conversation ended, I sensed that she had chosen 'Mary's' story because I needed to hear it. It was as if she saw the veil of my ignorance surrounding my relationship with my mother and was encouraging me to look beyond my confusion to the deeper practice of forgiveness.

I did not share my thoughts with Venerable Dhammananda that day but, if I had, I might have said something like this: *I am not ready to forgive my mother, I am still clinging to anger and resentment, but I understand what you are saying, and someday, with practice and understanding, I too will be able to heal my relationship with my mother.*

CHAPTER 3

The Turning Point

To confront any issue that is challenging you must have
your spiritual root – it is like a well you draw from.

A few months later, I visited the temple for the full moon ceremony also known as *Wan Phra* or Buddhist holy day. On holy days, we went on alms round at dawn and in the evening we gathered on the third floor of the main shrine to recite the Medicine Buddha chant 108 times. In the beginning I would hear myself chanting, but soon our voices blended into one, and I would float away on the sound, like being lifted on a cloud. Afterwards, we would form a circle and each person would say something about their day. Everyone loved this time because the sharing brought us closer together.

Venerable Dhammananda and I arranged to meet at lunchtime around 11.30 a.m. that day. The sound of the gong located next to the main shrine rang loudly – *tong-tong-tong* – announcing the midday meal. This was our signal to begin lunch and all the laypeople, me included, lined up along the far edge of a long metal table covered with appetizing food displayed in plates and bowls in different sizes and colours. The ordained women were seated with their alms bowls in front of them. Venerable Dhammananda sat at a separate table with various bowls of food placed in front of her.

The female nuns pressed their palms together and chanted the blessing for the meal. After their chant they quietly lined up by seniority, the woman who had been ordained the longest first in line followed by the women ordained more recently. Venerable Dhammananda remained seated while the other ordained women took their places opposite us on the other side of the metal table. As I'd been instructed, I bent over slightly along with the others, stretched my arms out, and touched the underside of the table with open palms. The nuns held their alms bowl in one hand and touched the underneath edge of the table with their other hand. With this simple gesture, the nuns accepted the food offered on the table by the laypeople and proceeded to serve themselves. Once the nuns were seated, the laypeople served themselves food.

At the monastery, meals are eaten in silence, so all I could hear was the faint tapping of the wooden chimes thumping in the breeze as I sat at a table with four other women. After eating, we each washed our own dishes in cold water and soap and lined them up to dry in dish racks.

I returned to my table and waited for Venerable Dhammananda to finish. People often came to kneel at her feet and speak with her after she ate, but no one approached her today. I watched her sweep her robe over her left shoulder and walk towards me with a purposeful stride.

Smiling, she said, 'Wait here a minute. I have a new book to show you.' She returned with the book, flipped through the pages, and pointed to a photograph of a mural in which two lines of women followed the Buddha in procession. 'These are the first women bhikkhunis ordained by the Buddha – they are the thirteen Arahat Theris. The volunteers at the National

Museum told me about this painting at Wat Po, near the ceiling behind the Buddha's head.'[28] I knew Wat Po, the temple famous for its statue of the reclining Buddha. I had no idea the painting was there but made a mental note to look for it on my next visit.

Beaming, she said, 'Now when people ask me, I can show them the picture. The reason I am standing here is because of these women. They are my spiritual root. The Buddha was the first one in world religions to say that men and women are spiritually equal. Do you know the story?'

I shook my head.

'When Queen Mahapajapati, the Buddha's aunt and stepmother, first came to the Buddha and asked him for permission to ordain, he refused her. But Queen Mahapajapati did not give up. She and her five hundred followers shaved their heads, donned the saffron robes, and followed the Buddha on foot to Vesali. They arrived covered with dust, their robes torn, their feet bleeding.

'Ananda, the Buddha's devoted disciple and assistant, learned about their dilemma and approached the Buddha on their behalf. Upon asking for permission a second time, the Buddha said no, but Ananda persisted. It was only when Ananda asked the Buddha whether his refusal was because women were not capable of achieving spiritual enlightenment that the Buddha made it clear that men and women had equal spiritual potential and he allowed women to be ordained. That was the golden phrase. Double underlined', she exclaimed. 'The Buddha said, "They can see it with their own eyes."'

I was impressed by Venerable Dhammananda's confidence. I now understood why she described the Buddha as the first feminist, because he declared women and men to be equal spiritually. I had often heard Venerable Dhammananda describe herself as a Buddhist and a feminist. I asked her what she meant.

Venerable Dhammananda said, 'In 1983 I was exposed to the feminist movement for the first time, a major turning point in my life. I was invited to speak at a conference at Harvard Divinity School on Women, Religion, and Social Change. My presentation was on the future of Theravada bhikkhunis in Thailand since I was the recognized authority on the subject.

'I had heard about feminism but had never experienced it. I was so inspired to be surrounded by forty strong feminists, some of them angry and militant. One woman had been jailed so many times her hair turned white. A woman from Latin America stood up and read an emotional poem. We all cried. I was shocked to hear the stories of women's suffering. It made a deep impression on me.'

Her brow furrowed. 'I felt conflicted about the militant feminists, they were so angry. I empathized with their cause but did not want to be angry like them. In Thai culture we do not confront or humiliate anyone publicly. Especially women. It is very difficult in Asian culture for women to speak up – to go against the status quo. If I behaved like the Western feminists, I would never achieve anything.'

By the second day of the conference, Venerable Dhammananda was emotionally overwhelmed and decided to take a break. She visited a museum and found a beautiful statue of Avalokiteshvara (the Bodhisattva of Compassion) sitting in a relaxed manner with one of his arms resting on his knee. Seeing that statue helped her recover.

Bodhisattva Avalokiteshvara in Water Moon form

Venerable Dhammananda declared, 'Harvard was a turning point for me because I transitioned from being an academic to an activist. Before the conference I was happy as an academic, sitting in an ivory tower away from the turmoil of the world. I asked myself, "What good am I?" I have studied Buddhism and the plight of the bhikkhunis. I have all this information but am not doing anything to improve the situation. I wanted to be more engaged and more involved in the struggle to ordain women as bhikkhunis in Thailand, but I did not like the suffering part. Some activists who work on social causes burn out because they see so much injustice.'[29]

Venerable Dhammananda looked directly at me as she spoke. 'If we hold so much on our shoulders, we suffer, and when we do, we are not helpful to anyone. I wanted to offer myself to society but was concerned about my happiness.

That is when I decided to come back to my Buddhist roots to anchor myself in peaceful thoughts. To confront any issue that is challenging you must have your spiritual root – it is like a well you draw from. It never dries up. Buddhism is such a great strength, a really great strength.'

This made sense and yet I wanted to understand her better. I asked, 'Can you give me an example of how you integrate feminism into your Buddhist practice?'

'I always say I am a Buddhist first, and a feminist second. Because of my training and my understanding of Buddhism, I emerged a better feminist. I wanted to be involved but in the Buddhist way, with loving-kindness, not hating those who did not agree with me or saw things differently.'

She looked thoughtful. 'I used to get very upset. I could feel my face get hot, becoming very angry when people confronted me. I examined myself closely and after going back to my practice, I realized I have more compassion for people who confront me. I understand their ignorance. Now, as a feminist I am not fighting against individuals, I am fighting against ignorance. Do you see?'

I nodded. The notion of combining feminist attitudes with loving-kindness made sense to me. I thought about my own reactions when someone disrespects me. I am much more prone to blame the person and fire back in anger. I have a difficult time maintaining my composure. I confessed to Venerable Dhammananda I am not very good at dealing with others when they are upset with me and end up reacting from a resentful place.

'The important question is how we choose to deal with life's painful experiences – a parent who mistreats us, an angry employer, or a disgruntled partner. Do we hang onto the negative mindset, or move into acceptance and forgiveness?' Venerable Dhammananda asked.

'I have an example from my own life I would like to share with you. It was 2001, the year after I was ordained, and as you know I received a lot of negative press. One local newspaper reporter was particularly disrespectful. He opposed my ordination, wrote false stories about me, insulted me, and called me "the bald-headed woman". I did not confront him at that time.

'When I returned to Thailand from Sri Lanka, after receiving full ordination in 2003, this same reporter was waiting for me at the airport. I was tired from the trip and did not want to deal with him. Somehow, I managed to avoid him and snuck back to the temple. However, when I arrived, he was there in the parking lot. I realized I could not run away from him. I walked straight up to him, looked him directly in the eye, and said, "What is there to write about? An old woman getting ordained. You do not need to be reporting on me." He did not have much of a reaction, but I knew I had made an impact.

'I learned a big lesson from this experience. I needed to face him. I was polite, speaking to him as if I were a grandmother speaking to a grandchild. This kind of motherly attention must have helped him come to his senses. The man never wrote about me again.'

Venerable Dhammananda was quiet, absorbed in her thoughts. Then she looked at me directly and said, 'Our conversation about feminism brings me back to my parents. I was moulded to be a strong and independent individual from my family upbringing. My mother was a very capable journalist and writer, also an accomplished jujitsu practitioner and sword fighter. In the summer of 1932, she rode her bicycle with the Boy Scouts from Bangkok to Singapore. It took her twenty-nine days. She brought me up to believe girls and women were equally as capable as men.'

I understood Venerable Dhammananda's connection to her mother but did not know anything about her relationship with her father. 'What was your father like?'

Venerable Dhammananda grinned. 'My father was the first feminist I ever met. He was a huge man, very hairy, typical of men who come from the south. He really liberated me from traditional female stereotypes by encouraging me to do whatever I wanted.'

Young Chatsumarn at age three pictured with her father, Koriet Shatsena

'Even though my parents separated when I was young, my father did visit me in Bangkok. He only stayed with us for about two weeks a year when Parliament was in session, so I did not see him very often. When I was twelve, he gave me my own camera and taught me to play golf before it was popular. He never let me get away with the excuse that I could not do it because I was a girl. He broke all the rules. When my mother came home and saw us playing cards or checkers, she disapproved of it, saying he was spoiling us.

'My father, Koriet Shatsena, was a dedicated politician who spent most of his life living and working on behalf of people living in southern Thailand. He was a member of the democratic party, which opposed the military-run government of the time. I admired his honesty; he was a righteous man who spoke up for the poor and openly criticized the government for its corruption. Because of his outspokenness he was imprisoned several times. I was always scared he was going to be taken to jail and because of that I shunned politics completely.'

Dhammananda threw her arms open wide. 'He was a joyful person with a loving heart. He gave us both his wealth and his debts. When my mother was ordained, the first time my father saw her, he bowed. He felt the revival of the bhikkhuni sangha was a question of social and religious equality. And then my father became a bhikkhu when he was fifty-eight.'

'How did your father decide to become a monk?' I asked.

'He decided to be ordained because of me. He loved me very much and when I asked him to become a monk, he agreed. By the time he was in his late fifties he had had enough of politics. He was a bhikkhu for eighteen years and towards the end of his life, when he could not take care of himself, he came to live with me here at the temple. I built him a *kuti* [small structure designed to house a monk] across the path from my house. He was seventy-seven when he died, and I planted a tree in his memory in front of where his *kuti* used to be. I walk by that tree every day and think of him.'

She spoke with a note of pride in her voice. 'I walked the soil of this country as the lone Theravada bhikkhuni thanks to my father who was a role model for protesting the system. I am grateful to my father's strong sense of encouragement and my mother's determination to create change. I inherited my sense of social responsibility from my father and my commitment to the monastic lifestyle from my mother.'

I could tell by the finality in Venerable Dhammananda's tone of voice that our conversation was ending. I thanked her and bowed in appreciation. Walking back to the car, I thought about the experiences she shared and was struck by her patience and compassion in dealing with her detractors. I had to admit it would be a challenge for me to approach my so-called 'enemies' with kindness. I was nowhere near ready to emulate her, but I could learn from her example. Perhaps the next time I got into an argument I would see the situation differently. I might not be able to forgive the person, but I could certainly take a moment to pause and reflect before launching into anger. I was grateful to my teacher, as always, for her guidance. She was helping me learn how to navigate life's difficulties with grace.

CHAPTER 4

Renunciation

You leave at the point you are most successful – that's renunciation.

On a December day, I continued my conversations with Venerable Dhammananda at the temple. I wanted to understand how, in her mid-fifties, she decided to renounce her worldly life – divorce her husband of thirty years, leave her three grown sons, and resign her position at a prestigious Thai university and as a TV host of a popular dharma show. She gave up a lot to become a Buddhist nun.

Arriving at the monastery, I peeled myself from the car seat and stepped out into the strong, mid-morning sun. Several barking dogs came up to greet me. These temple dogs knew instinctively to guard the nuns and bark at any strangers. I had learned it was best to walk away calmly and ignore them. Seemingly satisfied I was not a threat, they ran along about their business.

I checked in at the front desk and headed to the dining area where Venerable Dhammananda was seated at a metal table. She gestured, 'Come'. Together we walked into her office at the far end of the dining room, a tiny room with books and pamphlets stuffed into every corner. On the left side of her desk was a picture of her as a layperson seated next to her mother. There was quite a powerful contrast between the two women:

Venerable Voramai was plain and clean-shaven in her light-yellow robe, and her daughter wore red lipstick and makeup.

Venerable Dhammananda when she was still a professor, pictured with her mother

I knew Venerable Dhammananda had hosted a popular dharma show on Thai television before she was ordained. How, I wondered, did she go from being a celebrity of sorts to an ordained nun? I jumped right into the conversation.

'Your career was thriving – a TV celebrity, a respected professor, married with three sons – and you gave all that up to be ordained?'

'Yes. I was very successful, and there is always temptation for good money. Being a popular TV host was something I had never dreamed of doing. It all happened quite suddenly in 1993 in the aftermath of a monk scandal in Thailand. At the time, I had been teaching Buddhist Studies at Thammasat University for twenty years, and I was often called upon by the media to comment on current events pertaining to Buddhism.

'The monk scandal involved a handsome and charming Thai monk who was having affairs with foreign women. I'd been hearing rumours about him from colleagues in the academic community – one friend even sent me a copy of a tape-recorded phone conversation the monk had with one of the women. He was breaking his vows of celibacy. As the story spread and the press got word of it, the scandal became front-page news. The headlines dragged on for a year, and the Thai Sangha leadership was doing nothing about it. A group of nine academics convened to urge the Sangha to act. I was part of that group – and the only woman. It would take another full year before the Sangha finally decided to disrobe the monk.

'At the height of the media frenzy, I got a call from the TV show *Mong Tang Mum*, which means "different viewpoints". They wanted me to sit on a panel of four women to talk about the scandal. I was to give the point of view of a female Buddhist scholar. I loved public speaking and performed well. Soon after the show aired, a director from another show called *Life Is Not Without Hope* invited me to host their weekly dharma programme. They had seen me on the panel, and said they thought I was a talented presenter. I accepted their offer thinking it would be a one-time thing, not realizing they wanted me to host the show on an ongoing basis. The programme turned out to be a hit, and I was thrown into the spotlight overnight. Eventually, the show won an award for best dharma TV talk show.'

She smiled and tilted her head to the side. 'Then one day I was putting on my makeup, getting ready for the dharma show when, suddenly, I heard a voice in my head in English say, "How long do I have to do this?"' Venerable Dhammananda laughed. 'I used to be so happy putting on makeup. I wish you could see some of my lay pictures. I spent hours painting my nails and styling my hair. I had matching shoes and handbags for each outfit, and I wore a lot of jewellery. I enjoyed looking beautiful. I had achieved wealth, fame, everything, but at a point it was no longer fulfilling, and I needed a change.

'In Buddhism, we talk about renunciation. If I had waited until I was older, that is not renunciation. You leave at the point when you are most successful – *that* is renunciation. Do you remember the three brothers: greed, hatred, and delusion? I was grasping for wealth and success – grasping for I, me, mine. Letting go of grasping has a lot to do with not clinging to the self.'

I was confused by what she meant by the term 'self'. In an earlier lecture, I had heard her talk about the illusion of self and how the Buddha taught there is a middle path between the extremes of holding onto the self as real and completely denying the self. I asked her about this. 'You talk about the self not being real. Is the Cindy that sits here real?'

'Yes. Cindy is real, but this reality of Cindy is not permanent because we go through sickness and death. This self is real, but there is a limitation to that reality. Buddhism does not want us to hold onto this self as eternal and yet, we are not "no self". We have to understand what the Buddha was trying to tell us. If we go along blindly claiming there is no person here, people will think you are stupid, "How can you say that I am not sitting here?"'

I was relieved to hear this, and at the same time not entirely clear on the concept. Even so, I decided to let go of this discussion for the time being and return to our previous conversation about renunciation. I asked Venerable Dhammananda if it was hard to let go of her work and family.

She gazed directly at me with a thoughtful expression. 'Before I was ordained, I was desperately lonely. Even though I was surrounded by family, something was missing. Being a wife, mother, and professor was not enough anymore. I remember one evening, I was looking out the window and waiting for my sons to return home. I wondered, is this all there is? I felt empty inside and wanted to do something more meaningful with my life.'

I could not help thinking about my present situation. At that time, I was living as an ex-pat wife in Thailand in the privileged position of having a full-time domestic live-in helper, Durga, named for the Hindu mother goddess and warrior who sits atop a tiger. The Durga who worked for us was a one-woman army, spoke five languages, and was a phenomenal cook and house cleaner. I was a good cook, but once relieved of the duties, I rarely stepped into the kitchen. As for house cleaning, I was happy not to do it, but was feeling a bit lost since I was no longer needed in my domestic role.

I related to what Venerable Dhammananda felt and was looking to make changes. She was a powerful role model for me. I imagined it must have taken a lot of courage to risk losing everything she had achieved – career, family, and wealth. I was curious to know more about her process. When did she realize she wanted to be ordained? Was it difficult to tell her husband and sons? Was it lonely? I focused on one question at a time and asked how she decided to make a change.

'It was 1999, I was fifty-five years old, and everyone was excited about the new millennium. I wanted to mark the occasion by doing something memorable with my life, something auspicious that I could always look back on with pride.'

Her face lit up as she spoke about a workshop she attended three months before the millennium, where the teacher asked them to draw a river of life. 'I loved to draw and sketched the river. I drew a red dot to mark a special event that was happening in April of 2000. I had been thinking about participating in an upcoming ceremony in Taiwan where the Venerable Master Hsing Yun was offering the bodhisattva precepts to a group of laypeople. This was a huge event. You can't even imagine it – more than 3,000 people would be attending. I made the decision to go.'

Venerable Dhammananda grew quiet. 'You know, Most Venerable Master Hsing Yun passed away February 5, 2023, at the age of ninety-seven. I cannot put into words how great he was in his time. He came from China when he was about twenty years old and became a bhikkhu. Then he left China for Taiwan. He read the Buddhist sutras and brought the teachings to the larger community of laypeople in Taiwan. We are so grateful to him.

'He founded his temple, Fo Guang Chan in the southern part of Taiwan, the setting is so beautiful. He had a large and successful community of Chinese bhikkhunis. At one point there were 1,300 monastic members in the temple and 1,000 of them were bhikkhunis. He was always supportive of the revival of the bhikkhunis in Theravada Buddhism.

'Venerable Master Hsing Yun organized the international ordination ceremony for the bhikkhunis in India in 1998. I was invited to attend as a Buddhist scholar. I flew from Calcutta to Bodh Gaya, and it just so happened Master Hsing Yun was on the same flight. One hundred and forty-eight women from different countries were ordained in Bodh Gaya that year and among them were twenty candidates from Sri Lanka. Throughout his lifetime his mission was to help strengthen the fourfold Buddhist community and particularly the bhikkhunis.

'In Taiwan the bhikkhunis are strong role models for the community. They serve as deans of academic departments, and rectors in the universities. These women are socially engaged, and this all started with Venerable Master Hsing Yun who was so farsighted in his vision, and supported gender equality between the bhikkhus and bhikkhunis.'

Venerable Dhammananda became emotional. 'As bhikkhunis in Theravada Buddhism we are very grateful to Venerable Master for helping us to establish the present-day bhikkhuni sangha. We call him Venerable Grandfather. His life is legendary, he was a cornerstone of the new era to establish Buddhism in the East. He paved the way for us to emerge from many centuries of darkness into the light.'

Venerable Dhammananda was thoughtful. After a brief pause, she continued. 'Let me tell you about my experience in Taiwan receiving the bodhisattva vows.' She extended her left forearm and rested it on the table as she pointed to three, faded white dots. 'On the last day of the event, everyone came together in one large group. The main hall could not accommodate so many people, so we stood in line on the front lawn. The ceremony lasted late into the night and culminated in *Ran Xiang*, a ritual burn on the arm symbolizing our commitment to the Bodhisattva path.

'Participation in this ritual was optional. Those of us who wanted to be involved entered the main hall and stood in line at a table where a bhikkhuni drew three small circles in a row on our forearms. Next, we held our arms out, and another bhikkhuni came and placed three incense cones on the marks and lit them. Once the cones burned down to the skin, they were removed. We returned to the grassy area outside, where volunteers offered us thin watermelon slices to cool the burn. It was refreshing since it was still warm and humid, even late at night.

'I went back to my line to join the other women. They walked up to me and smiled. I couldn't understand the language they spoke, but their warmth was unmistakable, and their message was clear: they'd come to congratulate me. Before that, no one had said anything to me. Apparently, foreigners did not usually participate in *Ran Xiang*, so they were impressed. For the first time, they treated me like I belonged to their group, and that meant a lot to me.'

She touched her forearm, 'When I returned home to Thailand, the burns on my arm became infected, and I had to change the dressings every day for a month. My elder sister, who also lived at the temple, thought having my arm burned was a stupid thing to do, but I did not think so. For me, it was like an initiation, my first step on the spiritual path. I was questioning whether I could commit to the life of a Bodhisattva. The work of the Bodhisattva is much more than taking a burn; it involves a commitment to help others be happy, joyful, peaceful, and free from suffering.

'If I was too afraid to take a little burn, how could I be trusted to take on the burden of responsibility the Bodhisattva way of life entailed? These dots represented my commitment to serve others. The decision had to come from me. Once you choose to walk this path, you must let go of yourself as an individual and put the interest of others before you, the interest of the Buddha before you. By taking the Bodhisattva vows, you are no longer looking out for yourself, you are working on behalf of others, caring for society and for the world.'

I was inspired by what Venerable Dhammananda had shared and admired the depth of her commitment to serve others. I was about to ask another question when a tall Thai man with thick black curly hair popped his head in the doorway. He had a quiet manner and bowed deeply from his waist as a sign of respect to Venerable Dhammananda. She smiled, extending her hand in the young man's direction. 'This is Chattakur, my youngest son. He is an artist. Do you see the curtain behind me? Let me show you something.' She stood and opened the panels to reveal a painting of a beautiful woman with long ears, gold earrings, a gold necklace, and a gold headpiece. 'This is Tara, the Tibetan embodiment of wisdom.'

I looked up at the image. Robes of deep orange and light blue draped Tara's arms, and her right breast was exposed. Her right palm was open, and in her left hand she held the stem of a huge pink peony.

Venerable Dhammananda continued. 'Chattakur painted this picture, and he is working on another picture of the Green Tara for me.' They spoke for a few minutes in Thai, and I was struck by the respectful distance he maintained while they talked. He stayed in the doorway, yet there was an unmistakable bond between them and a motherly pride in Venerable Dhammananda's voice. After their brief conversation, Chattakur left.

Meeting her son made me think about my own family, how difficult it would be to leave them. I imagined what it would be like to leave my husband. We had been married for twenty years, and the thought of being alone terrified me. I believed that was something I would never be able to do. I wondered what it was like for Venerable Dhammananda and asked if it was hard to leave her husband.

She confessed to feeling conflicted. 'We had been married for more than thirty years. Even though I told my husband of my intention to become a monastic before we were married, he was surprised when I followed through. When I asked for a divorce, he was not angry, but confused. He had no objection to my being ordained, but asked, "Why the divorce?" Because he was in the military, it was a matter of saving face; he did not want to be humiliated by me in public.

'Eventually, my middle son, Vorachat, intervened on my behalf and talked to my husband. Out of my three sons, he is the one everyone respects. He's quiet, but when he speaks up, everyone listens. He asked me one question, "Did your mother force you to do this?"' I understood why he might ask this. Venerable Dhammananda said her mother controlled everything in the temple. It was easy to imagine that her mother might have pressured her to be ordained.

'"No", I answered. "It is my decision." After that Vorachat spoke to his father, who agreed to the divorce.'

I asked her why her husband agreed to her son's request, but not to hers when she first asked.

Venerable Dhammananda's eyes opened wide. 'I need to explain how things work in Thai culture. My husband was in the military. Typical of men in that profession, it would have been one thing if he asked me for a divorce, but it was quite another thing for me, a woman, to make such a request. In Thailand, there is a strong tradition of saving face, which means not confronting or publicly humiliating anyone. It is very difficult in Asian cultures for women to speak up and go against the status quo. It is not like in America, where women speak up all the time.'

I thought about this from the Asian perspective, and it made me realize all the social taboos Venerable Dhammananda faced – not only in being ordained, but by asking for a divorce in the first place.

Dhammananda mentioned that her sons supported her decision to be ordained, but that it was hardest on her eldest son. He said he had to sacrifice his mother to the Buddha and was sad he could not hug or touch her anymore. This was because Thai bhikkhunis cannot have any physical contact with members of the opposite sex. Venerable Dhammananda looked down and was silent. She seemed to need a private moment, so I remained quiet for a few minutes.

When she looked up, there was a softness in her voice as she shared that her eldest son had been going through some difficulties. She acknowledged, 'Sometimes it is hard to stay emotionally anchored when it is your own son.'

She struck me as incredibly vulnerable in that moment, so honest and open. I had never met a woman quite like Venerable Dhammananda – so powerful, yet so sensitive at the same time. Perhaps this was what drew me to her in the first place. I had been brought up to believe that the tougher you are, the more powerful you are. I had ingested society's notion that expressing emotions somehow made a person weak. When it came to feelings, I grew up thinking I was too sensitive, naive, and shared too much.

Over the years, Venerable Dhammananda shifted my understanding of what it means to be a woman. She is a living example that you can be both powerful and express the truth of your feelings – especially warmth and compassion. A role model, she has helped me embrace a new understanding of my own femininity – strength through vulnerability. This has been a valuable lesson and, over time, through my teacher's example, I have gained overall confidence in becoming more open, honest, and caring in my relationships with others.

CHAPTER 5

Ordained

You are walking against the tide of the river.
That's what Buddhists are meant to do.

As I drove towards the temple, I felt a familiar excitement and was eager to see Venerable Dhammananda again. By now she was used to my frequent visits, and I was amazed given her busy schedule that she always made time for me. It was about 2 p.m., the time she usually spent answering emails on her computer. I peeked into her office, but she was not there. I decided to take a short walk and headed to the spirit house to pay my respects.

The spirit house at the temple

Spirit houses are part of Thai culture based on the ancient religious practice of animism, which believes objects in nature, such as plants and trees, possess souls or spirits. Spirit houses, called *San Phra Phum*, meaning 'shrine of the guardian spirit', are placed outside Thai homes and businesses. People pay their respects to the spirits by lighting incense and offering food. It is believed that appeasing the spirits facilitates happiness, prosperity, and a peaceful life.

The temple spirit house is located midway between the front entrance and the gate to the back garden. Venerable Dhammananda once told me, 'Before Buddhism came to Thailand, we believed in spirits of the land. When we buy a piece of property and build a house, we also believe that there may have been a spirit taking care of the land before us, so we build a house for them. When visiting the temple, people light three sticks of incense and pay their respects, saying "May you be peaceful, may I be peaceful, may you protect me while I am staying here."'

I liked the idea of spirits living on the land, and every time I visited the temple I paid my respects. Today was no different; I stood in front of the spirit house, bowed three times, wished the spirits well, and then headed back to her office.

Venerable Dhammananda was there working at her computer, so I tapped lightly on the door frame to get her attention. She looked up and waved me in. Without hesitation she asked, 'What questions do you have for me today?'

I smiled and bowed. She knew me well. I returned to the topic of her ordination. 'I know that towards the end of 2000 you were deciding which lineage to ordain in – Tibetan, Mahayana, or Theravada Buddhism. You were very interested in the Tibetan lineage because of your close connection to His Holiness the Dalai Lama. What was your relationship like?'

Venerable Dhammananda was thoughtful as if she were reaching back into her memory to retrieve important details. 'The first time I met his Holiness was 1980. At that time, I devoted hours to translating his books from English to Thai. I translated *Freedom in Exile: The Autobiography of The Dalai Lama*, and seven other Tibetan books into Thai.

'I had a lot of faith in His Holiness' wisdom. In the early days it was easy to arrange an in-person meeting, so I travelled to Dharamsala, India to see him. I remember sitting in the waiting room next to his office before we met. I could hear him laughing next door, and his laughter was so contagious I could not help but laugh along with him. I was very happy.

'When they let me into the room I bowed on the floor, but he asked me to sit on a low chair. We talked for about an hour, mainly about the bhikkhuni issue, and he asked for a copy of my PhD dissertation on the Bhikkhuni Patimokkha [monastic rules]. I am sure he wanted to pass my research on to his advisers. At that time the Tibetan religion officials were only offering novice ordination to women, but they were considering higher ordination and my thesis provided valuable information in that regard.

'Toward the end of our session, I mentioned a pamphlet I had seen in the waiting room that talked about newly ordained monks, but not nuns. I gave him a small offering of about $300 to include something about Tibetan nuns. I was surprised when I returned the next year to see the same brochure printed with the word "nuns" inserted.'

She paused for a moment before continuing, 'Whenever I visited His Holiness, I felt as though I had been initiated into a new world, a new way of seeing, being and understanding everything around me.'

Venerable Dhammananda ultimately did not choose to be ordained in the Tibetan tradition because she would have had to remain a novice since higher ordination was not permitted. 'Thai people would have been confused', she said. 'First, I would wear the maroon robes, and then switch to orange. They would not understand.'

Venerable Dhammananda is unusual for a Thai Buddhist because she has studied the Tibetan and Mahayana branches, not just Theravada. The fact that she took the bodhisattva precepts in the Mahayana tradition from the Chinese Master Venerable Master Hsing Yun was just one indication of how open-minded she is. She placed a lot of importance in the bodhisattva practice of helping others to become free of suffering. Given that her mother was ordained in the Mahayana tradition, I wondered if Venerable Voramai influenced her decision. 'What about your mother? Did she have an opinion?'

'My mother wanted me to ordain in the Mahayana tradition in Taiwan, probably because she took full ordination there in 1971. However, by the time I was ready to be ordained she was already ninety-two years old and confined to bed by osteoporosis. She lived in an air-conditioned, free-standing glass room on the second floor of the main temple and was probably not aware that Theravada bhikkhuni ordination was possible in Sri Lanka. Eventually, I decided not to ordain in the Mahayana tradition because I did not read Chinese, so I would not have been able to study the texts. That is when I began to think seriously about being ordained in the Theravada tradition.'

I asked Venerable Dhammananda to describe her ordination experience in 2001.

'My close Sri Lankan friend, Ranjani de Silva, made all the arrangements for me and told me what to expect. Two of my graduate students took me to the airport. Only a few friends and my family knew what I was about to do. I wanted to maintain a low profile and not attract too much attention to myself.'

She arrived at Sakyadhita Meditation Centre in Panadura, Sri Lanka. 'The morning of my novice ordination I met my Sri Lankan *pavattini* [a senior female monastic teacher also called 'preceptor'], Venerable Saddha Sumana, for the first time. I knew about her because she was one of the original twenty Sri Lankan women ordained in 1998 in Bodh Gaya. Prior to ordination, she had been a *dasa sil mata* [ten precept novice] for more than forty years.' Venerable Dhammananda added, '*Dasa sil mata*s are like Thai *mae chi*s.'

'I was staying at the Sakyadhita Centre south of Colombo in Sri Lanka.' A photograph was taken of Venerable Dhammananda and her teacher, Venerable Saddha Sumana, in the garden of the Centre. Venerable Dhammananda was seated under the *nag* tree with its delicate blossoms.

'Venerable Saddha Sumana did not speak much English and I did not speak Sinhalese. We did not say much; she pulled a pair of scissors out of her pocket and began trimming my hair.

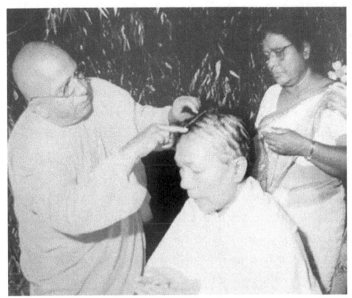

Venerable Dhammananda with Venerable Saddha
Sumana on the morning of her novice ordination

'The blades were too dull to cut smoothly, but Venerable
Saddha Sumana did not seem to notice. When I looked at the
scissors, I was shocked. They were all rusty, so my teacher had a
difficult time grabbing my hair. At one point I felt a sharp pain
on my head and flinched; she had nicked my scalp. A young Sri
Lankan bhikkhuni who was assisting us ran to get toothpaste
to stop the bleeding. They used a razor blade to shave my head,
there was no electric shaver. Had I known they did not have the
proper tools I would have brought my own clippers with me.'

I asked Venerable Dhammananda if she was upset.

She laughed and said, 'No. What could I do? I covered my
newly exposed scalp with a white cloth, and we headed over to
Tapondanramaya temple for the ordination ceremony, about a
twenty-minute drive from Sakyadhita Centre.

'When I arrived at the temple, Venerable Dhammaloka, the senior monk in charge, asked me to raise the Thai flag. I did not understand why, until he explained that I was exactly like Venerable Princess Sanghamitta of ancient times who had brought the bhikkhuni lineage from India to Sri Lanka in the third century. Like Princess Sanghamitta, I was bringing the bhikkhuni lineage from Sri Lanka to Thailand. We hoisted three flags that day, Sri Lankan, Thai, and Buddhist. It was a huge honour for me.'

Venerable Dhammananda paused to take a sip of water. 'Ranjani led me to the ordination hall for the ceremony. Five senior monks trained in the *Syamvansa* [Thai lineage] tradition had been invited to give me samaneri ordination. I was sweating profusely because there was no electricity or fans in the hall. Not that it bothered me, I was too excited to care. Venerable Saddha Sumana took a cushion next to me. We sat cross-legged side by side on the floor. I thought we would have time to rehearse beforehand but was quite surprised to find out the ceremony began right away.

'The monks started to chant, and my heart raced because I did not understand what was going on. When my teacher wanted me to stand, she pulled me up, and when she wanted me to sit, she yanked me down. I was so nervous, not knowing what to do. Thankfully, I made it through the ceremony and, at the end, made my way to Venerable Dhammaloka who was seated on the floor. I bowed three times to pay my respects. He handed me my robes, neatly folded in a packet. Ranjani ushered me out of the hall to a side room where I changed into my robes. We headed back to the hall where I received ordination and took the precepts. It all happened so fast I did not have time to register my feelings.

'After the ceremony I approached Venerable Dhammaloka and told him I had chosen my ordained name. I took the first part – Dhamma – to honour him, and the second part of my name – Nanda – because it referred to Mahapajapati's daughter, the princess named Nanda, which meant "the beautiful one". I took her daughter's name to be reminded that I, too, am a daughter of Mahapajapati; she is my spiritual root.'

Venerable Dhammananda did not see herself shaved until later. 'The day of my ordination was long, and I was very tired. I went to sleep and had one of the deepest sleeps of my life. When I got up, I went into the washroom. I happened to walk past the sink and above the sink was a mirror. I should have thought I looked strange with my head shaved, but instead I thought, *I have seen you before*. It was that kind of feeling and not a shock.'

Venerable Dhammananda looked down thoughtfully. 'I had an emotional reunion with my mother when I returned to Thailand. I approached her quietly. Her health was failing, and she was bedridden. I asked her what she thought of my ordination. She simply stroked my face, playing with my head as if to confirm it was really shaved. After a while, she let me go as she always did. Since I wore the holy robes, however, she gestured in a *wai* – joining her palms in front of her chest – as a sign of respect to me.'

Venerable Dhammananda lowered her voice and continued, 'I led a very quiet life after I returned to Thailand, but not for long. News of my ordination hit the front pages in April of 2001. I was invited to give an interview about my ordination on a TV channel that was controlled by the military. The day of the interview, they cancelled the show. Up to this point, my ordination had not attracted so much attention, but once they cancelled the show the fact that they censored it became a huge issue for the next few weeks. The media got involved and wanted to know why it was cancelled.'

I was amazed to hear this. I assumed people had heard about Venerable Dhammananda's ordination and that was why there was such a negative backlash. But it turned out the whole debate escalated, in part, because of one cancelled interview.

Venerable Dhammananda leaned forward with a serious expression. 'For more than three months I was front page news. Apart from my mother, I was literally standing alone.'

'Were you surprised at the reaction you received?'

She sighed. 'I knew there would be a negative response but did not realize it would be so strong. During my mother's time, she received criticism, but the media was not so powerful. When I was ordained, the media had a bigger presence and also there was the internet. I did not browse the internet, but apparently there was a site focused on the issue of my ordination. I was not aware of it until, one day, a student of mine in the US alerted me to the controversy. I went online and saw many people were talking about me, saying crude and hostile things like I was ruining Buddhism. I could not get involved in that, so I left a message saying "I am the ordained person and if you care about Buddhism as much as you say you do, here is my address. Please come and visit me and see how we run the temple." People responded with what you call "spicy talk" but eventually the person hosting the programme shut the site down because they did not get another response from me. After that I kept quiet because I understood how the media distorts things.'

Venerable Dhammananda spoke with conviction, 'But I survived. So, when people say I am a revolutionary, of course, I am because I follow in the footsteps of the Buddha. You are walking against the tide of the river. That is what Buddhists are meant to do.'

Before I could respond to all she had said, the gong rang, signalling it was time for us all to meet in the garden. We congregated there every day at 4 p.m.

'Come.' She gathered her robes. 'We will do chi gung.'

There was a finality in her voice. She was ready to move on. Venerable Dhammananda had an uncanny ability to stay rooted in the present moment.

I did not have time to process all she had said, but there was an unmistakable teaching in her example that pointed to a familiar theme: do not hold on to the negative mindset. What happened in the past was done, let it go. Still, the words 'standing alone' echoed in my mind. For me, she was a truly courageous role model for women who faced injustice and took a position, a powerful example for all of us about how we each have moral agency and can effect positive change through our actions.

PART II
Heart-to-Heart Wisdom

The conversations presented in this section are gathered from personal interactions I had with Venerable Dhammananda and guests who have appeared on Casual Buddhism, a virtual programme I created in April 2021 in response to the COVID pandemic. People were feeling isolated and in need of spiritual connection, so I invited guests to speak one-on-one with Venerable Dhammananda over Zoom. The programme offered people in the West a rare opportunity to connect with a senior Asian Theravada Buddhist teacher.

Our guests have included well-known meditation teachers, friends, and students of Buddhism who discuss their spiritual practice with Venerable Dhammananda. Often, they ask a question, and she responds. Because of her sincerity and warmth, Venerable Dhammananda establishes trust and rapport with people, and they experience a renewed sense of hope after their conversations with her. Use this link to connect with Casual Buddhism: https://www. youtube.com/@casualbuddhism

'With our breath we care for the world.' Venerable Dhammananda speaking at the temple in 2007

CHAPTER 6

Meditation

My exhalation is your inhalation.

One morning while at Venerable Dhammananda's temple I decided to meditate in the Medicine Buddha *Vihara* (shrine). I've always had profound experiences when I sit with the Medicine Buddha. There is something about being in the presence of this majestic Buddha that inspires me to go deeper in my practice.

Medicine Buddha

Even though Venerable Dhammananda is a Theravada Buddhist, early on she became interested in the Medicine Buddha, a Mahayana deity, and a powerful healer:

> In 1994 when she was still a professor teaching Buddhist studies at Thammasat University, Venerable Dhammananda was sitting in meditation and saw the image of a full-bellied Chinese healing Buddha sitting cross-legged in a beautiful valley with mountains around him. His kneecap had a flap-door where people could enter his body. At the time, she did not understand what the vision meant.
>
> In the next three years after she had the vision, Venerable Dhammananda traveled to many countries searching for the Buddha image she had seen in her meditation. In Myanmar and Taiwan, she asked healing masters if they could direct her to what she was looking for. She never found the Buddha and only understood what her meditation meant after she was ordained in 2001 when she realized she was supposed to build her own sanctuary for the Medicine Buddha where sick people could come and pray.[30]

She drew a sketch of the Medicine Buddha like the one in her meditation and gave it to a local sculptor. It took one year for him to create a finished wax model from her drawing. The Medicine Buddha in the back garden is 3.2 metres tall and the width at his knees is 2.7 metres. He is made of brass and his crown and forehead are covered in gold. Lay members of the temple donated their gold earrings and chains to be melted down for the Buddha's head.

The Medicine Buddha Vihara is located at the far end of the temple garden. To get there I walked behind the dormitory along a path that led to the back gate. I always rushed past this one particular spot holding my breath, because of the stench from an open drain at the base of the wall. That day, despite the acrid smell, I slowed down and noticed there was writing on the wall to my left. I stopped to read the neat script in Thai and English. There were twelve different sayings written side by side, and one in particular caught my attention: *As a brown leaf falls it belongs neither to the tree nor the ground*. I liked the thought but did not understand the meaning. I mentioned this to Venerable Dhammananda the next time I saw her. She looked surprised and said, 'Oh, no one has ever noticed that before. In this one I was thinking about meditation. When you meditate you should be free from the past and the future. You are here in the present moment. Our life is so transient, like a falling leaf that belongs neither to the tree nor the ground.'

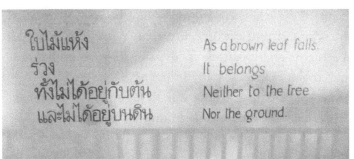

Dhammananda's reflections on meditation

I asked Venerable Dhammananda a simple question, 'Why is it important to meditate?'

She leaned forward with interest. 'If we look closely at our lives, most of us are searching for happiness, but as it happens, we often end up chasing it in the wrong places. We work so hard to earn money to allow us to travel to other countries in search of happiness. But we don't find happiness in the outer world. Happiness resides in the quality of our own mind, and we find it by turning inward.'

'Buddhism is unique among world religions because it provides so many different techniques to train the mind. The Buddha was so beautiful, he recognized people have individual needs and provided at least forty-six types of mental training that fall into two major categories. One is *samatha*, which is calm concentration, and the other is *vipassana*, which is insight meditation. Concentration is an important foundation for vipassana meditation. To be enlightened, you need to follow the path of vipassana meditation.'

I was confused about two similar sounding words, *samadhi* and *samatha*, and asked Venerable Dhammananda to explain the difference.

'Samadhi is when your mind is one-pointed or focused, whereas samatha means concentration. You need samadhi in both samatha and vipassana meditation. The mind has to be anchored before it can do anything else.'

Venerable Dhammananda was thoughtful for a moment. 'People often have the misconception that concentration is less important than vipassana and is not a necessary step along the path to enlightenment. But that is not totally correct. Concentration (samatha) is an important preparation for insight meditation because unless or until the mind is calm or concentrated, it is very difficult to proceed on to vipassana or insight meditation.'

She leaned forward with interest. 'Let me give you an example. A man walks through the forest in search of enlightenment. He carries with him a blunt knife, but the knife is so dull he can't cut the vines and branches blocking his way. So, no matter how sincere his intention, he cannot get through the jungle. Samatha is like a sharpened knife; it is the tool that allows you to walk through the forest. When your mind is trained in concentration, it becomes powerful, and you can clear the mental obstacles that bind you.

'We begin to practise meditation starting first with concentration. Vipassana starts when you begin to contemplate the truth of whatever mind-object you are concentrated on. The Buddha taught that all phenomena, including thoughts, emotions, and experiences, are marked by three characteristics: *anicca* (impermanence), *dukkha* (suffering), and *anatta* (no real self).

'You can look at the flame of a candle and when your mind is concentrated, you enter the next stage of clear seeing. "Ah!" you say, "The nature of the flame is such that it flickers." Indeed, you recognize its impermanence, it cannot stay, and has no real substance unto itself.

'The purpose of insight meditation is to allow you to let go, not of the world, but let go of clinging to the self which from the very beginning is not there. We have been clinging to this shadow of the self which we believe is real.' She pressed her lips together. 'When your mind has this understanding, you are doing vipassana, insight meditation. You can let go of clinging to whatever obstacles emerge in your practice. With insight meditation we begin to free ourselves from that which binds us to suffering. For a short period of time, we begin to experience this freedom, it is only temporary, yet we know what the Buddha taught can be real. It was real for him and can be real for us.'

I asked Venerable Dhammananda if she could offer a basic meditation practice to help me understand the difference between samatha and vipassana.

'Sure', she agreed. 'But before we begin, let me say a couple of things about practising meditation.'

'Let me tell you a secret about the mind: it can only concentrate on one thing at a time. We start meditating by following our breath. This breathing in and out is your life. Simply watch your breath. The mind will wander because we have not trained our mind – it is only natural that it behaves this way. Just note it. We do not embellish it or entertain it. Neither do we judge it harshly. Accept it. If a thought arises, we say, "Oh there you are! I recognize you." And it disappears by itself.

'There are many meditation techniques, but I would like to begin with a simple exercise called mindfulness of breathing; breathing is something we do all the time and have done ever since we were born. Usually, we take our breath very much for granted. In this meditation we practise observing our breath as though we were watching somebody else breathe. Thoughts will arise, and that is okay. Do not get caught up in them. Recognize each thought and simply put it aside. You may hear sounds like traffic or street noises, and that is fine. Let it go.'

She continued with her instructions:

- First, prepare to meditate. Sit cross-legged with your right leg on top of the left, or comfortably in a chair with both feet flat on the floor. Put your right hand on top of the left with your two thumbs touching in the middle. The left hand is your eyes, your ears, your nose, your tongue, your body. The right hand is the mind that supports the five senses.

- Be mindful that your back is straight. Tilt your head forward slightly as if you were looking about one foot in front of you. Place the tip of your tongue forward on the upper palate of your mouth. Close your eyes.

- As you breathe in, take in air to nourish yourself. Place your awareness, gently, at the tip of your nose. Watch the air touching the area below your nostrils and above your upper lip. Follow the inhalation and exhalation. Keep mindfully watching your breath move in and out. Eventually your body will become still, and you will calm down.

- Continue this for a while and you will observe your breathing become softer and softer until you can no longer feel it, and this means you are about to enter the concentration stage.

- When you are ready, shift your attention to the pause occurring before each inhalation and exhalation. Notice how the inhaling stops before the exhaling and vice versa. Each one depends on the other. Do you see it now? This is *samadhi*, or one-pointed concentration. You may simply want to stay here if you like, for thirty minutes or longer, it is so pleasant.

- Then we come to the realization that life is so fragile, we all depend on breathing in and out. That which is dependent falls into three characteristics: *anicca* (impermanence), *anatta* (no real self), and *dukkha* (dissatisfaction or suffering).

- With this understanding you have shifted from samatha to vipassana meditation. Continue meditation for as long as you like. When you are ready, slowly open your eyes and look around at your surroundings.

Venerable Dhammananda looked at me. 'Okay? You get the idea now?'

I understood, but admitted, 'My meditation practice is pretty basic. I always come back to my breathing when my mind is cluttered.'

Venerable Dhammananda nodded in agreement. 'Meditation is all about breathing', she said, confidently. 'When we breathe in, we take in air to nourish ourselves. When we breathe out warm air, we share loving-kindness and compassion with others, wishing them well. We need time to be with our breath without thinking. When we start to worry, do not get upset or have expectations, just note it. Simply stay with your breath, be in the present, be in the now. When we breathe deeply, we nurture and heal ourselves. When we experience this loving-kindness with ourselves, we can share it with others. With our breath we care for the world.'

'That is amazing! I never thought of my breath as a way of connecting to others.'

'Yes', she said. 'Your breathing out is my breathing in, and my exhalation is your inhalation. So, we all are connected from the very beginning. We have this illusion – this *maya* – that we are separate, but in fact, from the very beginning we are breathing the same air. We are all depending on each other.

That is why we must take care of the air, less pollution, we start looking at things in a more global way.'

'We are so interconnected', I muttered to myself.

'Yes!' she exclaimed. 'We each depend on one another. Imagine, if I am very grouchy, I am creating a negative vibration that affects you. I am not saying a word, but you see by my expression I am grumpy. We react to each other by the way we look. I always have a serious expression on my face at the temple, and people get scared.' She laughed. 'I say, "*My gosh, I have not done anything yet.*" People respond, "Venerable Mother, it is just the way you look." So, you see, Cindy, how we have to be responsible for the world.'

There was a pause in our conversation. Venerable Dhamma-nanda tilted her head in earnest and said, 'Let me come back to your question of breathing and to our earlier conversation about different meditation practices. Whatever meditation style you decide to practice, mindfulness must be present.'

The word 'mindfulness' sparked my attention. Everyone talks about it these days. Now that it has gone mainstream it means different things to different people, so I asked Venerable how she defined it.

'When our minds are fully present', she responded. 'When we are being mindful, we give our full attention. It is only when we are free of the past and the future that we can truly connect with people in the present time. Like right now, I am one hundred percent with Cindy. I watch your facial expressions carefully, are you upset, confused? Look at your eyebrows – are you puzzled, not understanding – all that. How often do we find ourselves engaged in conversation but not really listening to the other person? Conversely, how often do we really feel heard?

'Like I said, most of the time we are preoccupied with our thoughts. But there is a practice called "deep listening" when we empty our minds and truly listen to what the other person is saying. Deep listening can be part of a meditation practice because we are listening without judgement. This process involves letting go of ourselves and giving our full attention to the other person.

'You know how, when someone comes to us with a problem, we usually react right away? Our response is not coming from a place of truly understanding the teaching. When a person wants to talk, you need to allow them the space to express their feelings. We always react before we hear their last sentence and make a judgement. Maybe we can help this person by not saying anything at all. All these years, no one is really listening.'

Venerable Dhammananda shook her head and laughed. 'I see myself doing this all the time. *Why don't you do this? Why don't you do that?* I am not really listening to the other person's perspective. They are in a very different situation than I am. Deep listening is hearing the other person without that "I" judging them, because when we are in our judgemental mind we are too self-centred to truly respect another person's experience. We must remove ourselves to understand another person's suffering. This emptying ourselves is a deep practice, a serious practice to listen to the other person who is speaking to us.

'I freely admit this is hard for me. When I am with my adult children, I find myself growing impatient, reacting to what they are saying rather than listening. Sometimes when a person has shared deeply, we can simply sit in silence, take their hand, squeeze it and say, "Yes, I understand your suffering."'

Venerable Dhammananda Speaking about Meditation

The Buddha realized that the most important thing is the mind. You have the mind, the speech, and the body. The mind leads our speech and action. It is possible for all of us to practise meditation to get to know our own mind, to know our own mental behaviour so that we can control the mind in the direction that we want.

Many people talk about practising meditation. The word 'practise' is from Pali, *patipatti*, which means method. Therefore, for us to practise we are not looking at other people or outside ourselves, but looking inward, inside ourselves. We are looking at our mental formation, the way our mind works.

When we meditate, we try to see the mind in its original state before it starts functioning. The mind is so active all the time, it is difficult to see this. Now, talking about the mind, there are two qualities I would like to mention. First, there is the knowing mind which is the mind in its original state. The nature of knowing mind is to simply note or know things as they are. Second, there is the thinking mind. Our mind is so accustomed to thinking all the time, it is difficult to allow space for the knowing mind.

'What we usually see when we meditate is the functioning mind. It is compared to a torch light, we do not see the torch light, but we see the object which the light shows us. We see the mind's activities and watch it functioning. But when we remain calm and quiet, we are truly in samadhi, and we get a glimpse of the original mind. Our intention is to let go of suffering, to experience the mind as it is, before it starts reacting to messages you receive through your eyes, ears, nostrils, etc. Occasionally we get a glimpse of the mind in its original state, and when we come to this realization it is a very beautiful moment.'[31]

We are all familiar with the thinking mind – I am seventy-eight and have a very busy mind, thinking, thinking, all the time. When I am caught up in thinking I am not allowing the space for the original nature of mind to simply note things as they are. The thinking mind causes so much suffering, so much hatred, so much jealousy. But the nature of the knowing mind is such that it expands and includes everything and everyone. Once we allow the knowing mind to start working, there is no attachment, there is no Dhammananda, no Cindy. The attachment to I, me, my, mine simply falls away and allows you to experience that beautiful nature, with the big N.

So many people tell me, 'Venerable I cannot meditate, my mind is like popcorn, thinking all the time.' That is why so many teachers compare the mind to a wild monkey, because it is moving so fast in so many directions. But even the wild monkey can be trained. In Southern Thailand we have schools for training the monkey to climb the coconut tree and pick coconuts for us. They use their legs to twist the coconut and throw it down for the owner to pick it up. If we can train the wild monkey, there is no reason we cannot train the mind. Once our mind is trained, we can dictate it to our will.

When the Buddha walked his last journey, he was accompanied by Ananda. Every place he stopped, the monks and his followers knew that the Buddha had decided to pass away. It is important to follow his teaching closely. He spoke only about the importance of *sila* (morality), *samadhi* (one-pointed concentration), and *panna* (wisdom). The purpose of meditation is to purify the mind, and the intention of meditation is to lessen our mental defilements (greed, anger, and delusion) so that we can reduce our suffering and walk towards the path of enlightenment.

You can visualize the Buddha's teaching by drawing a circle. Put sila, samadhi, and panna in the centre and draw the eightfold path around it. Underneath panna (wisdom) you have sammadhitti (right view and right thought). This is panna.

Next is sila. You need morality, right speech, right action, and right livelihood to do the meditation properly. Our speech and body are pure because we are practising the five precepts. We don't steal, don't kill, don't commit sexual misconduct, lie, or use harsh speech, or use intoxicants. The five precepts keep us stable and provide a wholesome state of mind to meditate. *Kusala* is the Pali word for wholesome; our intention must always be wholesome when we sit down to meditate. The practice of samadhi comes about through right effort, right mindfulness, and right concentration. Meditation will bear fruit only when the sila is pure – sila, samadhi, and panna are taken together with the eightfold path.

When we sit in meditation, we practise concentration (samatha) so that we can have one-pointed mind (samadhi). In this deeper state of meditation, wisdom (panna) arises – wisdom about life and the Buddha's teachings. 'This one-pointed mind reveals that when you experience samadhi there is no "YOU" and there is no "I". There is no separate universe, it is all one. You, I, universe becomes one. The deeper the meditation, the more you realize the connectedness of everything on earth.'[32]

One-pointed mind is very powerful; it is where the mind becomes calm, peaceful, and bright. You become very rooted in yourself. When I speak, I speak with my whole body. I am really concentrated and speak with the power of my mind. When the mind is powerful enough, we can decide to do insight meditation – to walk through the forest and clear the mental defilements which cause so much suffering. We can free ourselves from clinging to I, me, my, mine, clinging to that self which is actually a shadow.

CHAPTER 7

Compassion

Everything begins here in our hearts.

In the years since I have known Venerable Dhammananda, we have spent many hours talking about compassion. She has helped me understand there is no magic formula to learn how to be more compassionate – our practice leads us on the pathway of discovery. During an episode of Casual Buddhism, I asked her about a phrase I had heard her repeat many times: *Everything begins here in our hearts.*

'Yes', she said, draping her robe over her left shoulder. 'Compassion begins from our heart first. When I feel compassion, my heart softens and when my heart is soft I am truly open to my shared connection with others. The Buddhist text refers to the person who cannot bear to see another suffer as the heart of *mahapurisa* which means "the great being".

'Compassion is when we reach out to help another person who is suffering. You do not think about yourself, you just react, you spring into action. Like when you see another person drowning, you jump into the river to help, but because you cannot swim you grab a piece of rope or something to pull them in.

'Let me give you another example. During the pandemic we had a project at the temple called Healing the Heart. I started this programme in response to a government announcement that they were giving 5,000 baht ($144.00) per month to poor families. I realized the poorest of the poor could not go online to sign up for the programme because they did not have computers or mobile phones. They did not have an ID to register or a bank account or an address because they lived in sheds. I decided to do something about this and donated temple funds to the poor.'

Venerable Dhammananda paused to collect her thoughts. 'We knew one woman who was very assertive and showed initiative, but she was suffering. She had to support her sister and take care of her mother who was bedridden. When the lockdown happened, she wanted to start a new business. Everything fell apart. She had no way to support herself. I gave her 5,000 baht right away just to help. Then, we began offering financial help to other members of the community. I asked trustworthy temple volunteers to hand out cash to the poor. Eventually, we helped fifty families, giving them 5,000 baht each for three months – the same amount they would have received from the government. I wanted to capture that feeling for you – when you cannot bear to see someone suffer.'

She focused her attention and said, 'You know about the four *brahmaviharas*?' Brahmavihara is derived from the Pali word *brahma*, meaning God or divine, and *vihara* meaning abode; taken together they mean divine abode. The brahmaviharas are also known as the four sublime states: *metta* (loving-kindness), *karuna* (compassion), *mudita* (joy), and *upekkha* (equanimity). I am speaking now about the first two states: loving-kindness and compassion.

'People sometimes confuse loving-kindness with compassion. Loving-kindness is often paired with compassion, but they are different. Loving-kindness is a wish for all beings to be happy, and compassion is a wish for all beings to be free from suffering. When you see someone in pain, you open your heart and there is no boundary between you and the other person. When that wall of separation falls away there is no self. When you feel another person's pain as if it were your own and you want to reach out to help, that is compassion. By helping others, we heal ourselves.'

I understood the helping part but was confused about how we heal ourselves. 'Can you give me an example?'

'Yes', she said. 'Suppose I know a husband and wife who are suffering. They are not getting along. I need to do something. Number one is to heal myself. I feel concerned for them and want to act on that – compassion expresses itself through action. I go see them and offer my support. Once I have done that, I feel satisfied. I cannot control the outcome but am content that I have tried my best.

'I'll give you another example. If a woman in our community is ill with cancer, I go visit her because if I don't, I feel worse. Again, by helping her, I am healing myself. Otherwise, I would experience *dukkha* (suffering). People might say, "Oh, Venerable Dhammananda is so full of compassion." *No!* Venerable visits the sick woman because if not, Dhammananda herself will suffer. That is the true expression of karuna.'

I thought about the fact that Venerable was constantly in a position of helping others. 'As a monastic, you have dedicated your life to caring for others. Do you ever feel overwhelmed? Is it sometimes difficult for you?'

'Oh yes, I really need to be strong within myself. It is not being self-centred, it is simply understanding that when we take better care of ourselves, we are better able to take care of others. Let me give you an example.

'I decided to ordain because of my great faith in the Buddha; it was he who established the fourfold Buddhist communities. My faith in him is one hundred per cent, and because of that, I abide by his teachings and trust his path is the right way forward. Many people around me opposed my ordination, but I was like a rock. I was very stable and knew that my decision was rooted in my faith.

'My intention to receive ordination was clear. I was not doing it for myself but taking the first step so that other women could follow. Suppose after I was ordained no one had followed me and I had been unable to form the bhikkhuni sangha? That would have been fine because I had done my best. When we are trying to help someone, but that person is not willing to help her- or himself, eventually we must step back and let go. Otherwise, we get thrown off by the other person and that is not being kind to ourselves.'

Venerable Dhammananda's face softened. 'If I am feeling weak emotionally, overburdened by something, or unbalanced, then I probably should not be trying to help someone else. I need to be fully anchored within myself.'

Venerable Dhammananda nodded. 'You must have panna [wisdom] or you will drown. I will give you an example from nature. If you watch a bird, the bird will teach you that if one wing is not working, the bird cannot fly. Compassion is only one wing of the bird; the other wing is wisdom. In terms of practising compassion, it is helpful to understand that both wings need to be balanced for the bird to fly.'

She lifted her head with assurance. 'We simply cannot afford to be compassionate to others all the time. Too much compassion can be harmful. For example, as you know, right after I returned from my novice ordination in Sri Lanka there was a huge uproar in the media. People said negative things about me behind my back, so I had to be tough. There was one young female reporter who was nice to my face and called me "Luang Mae" which means Venerable Mother. "Oh, Venerable Mother, this person said this about you, what do you think?" I would react right away, and she would go back to the other person and say "Dhammananda said this about you." That person would make a negative comment, and she'd come back to me and ask, "What is your reaction?"

'It went back and forth like this for a while and the more I talked the worse it got. She played us against one another and of course the newspapers sold very well. I was being used and decided to stop talking to the media altogether. I learned a lot from my experience. With our wisdom we ask ourselves, is this the time? Shall we wait? What shall our response be? We balance our compassion with wisdom.'

She closed her eyes in silent contemplation as if to gather her energy. Then she opened her eyes and continued, 'It is important to understand that before we can have compassion for others, we must first have compassion for ourselves. The Buddha said, "Be beneficial to yourself and be beneficial to others." One way to nurture self-compassion is through our breath. Before I can care for you, I have to breathe in, and with that breath I nourish my soul and body. When I breathe out, I am sharing that nourishment, the good feeling from my heart to yours, it goes like that.

'We nourish ourselves by breathing deeply. We must be kind to our physical self, we have mistreated our bodies for so long. Often we take short, shallow breaths because we want to please others, we worry about what others think and who they expect us to be. We are not even breathing properly, and it becomes a habit to breathe halfway.'

Venerable Dhammananda spoke more intimately. 'Many of us try to be polite in life. We are encouraged to take care of others, often at the expense of ourselves. We behave according to social protocols without respect to ourselves. I say this because I have been through that. We need to realize it is not good for us. We can be true to ourselves and still be polite to others.'

Her voice softened, 'No one explained this to me and for many years my breath was quite shallow because I was afraid of so many things. I was not being sincere with myself.'

I was curious and asked, 'What were you afraid of?'

'It has a lot to do with being a Thai woman: you do not speak up in public. Whether right or wrong, you're supposed to crawl on your knees. From an early age I was taught to be polite, so many social rules telling me what I was not supposed to do. Even laughing out loud was not considered polite behaviour for a "lady". I was worried about doing or saying the wrong thing. My body was so tense I could not even relax and breathe normally.'

Venerable Dhammananda looked pensive. 'It took me a long time to release my fear about going against the social norm, but through the years I gained experience and education, and met more people. Once I was exposed to the larger world, I became less fearful. I did not have to burden myself anymore with social expectations. Mine was a slow process from that young woman to Dhammananda... a long time.

'You know, Cindy, the kind of life we lead now is full of stress. No wonder cancer is the number one illness we are facing. The stress we have is caused by our own way of thinking.

'So, number one, be kind to yourself. Love yourself more. Loving yourself seems as though it is easy, but it isn't when you practise it at a higher level. Many of the things that bother us are rooted in the fact that we do not truly understand how to love ourselves. This loving ourselves comes back to focusing on our breath, especially during meditation. When you meditate, sit in a relaxed, comfortable position. Take in a deep breath to nurture your physical body and allow yourself to enjoy that. We can use our breath as a checkpoint to see if we are okay – whether we are breathing normally and taking good care of ourselves.'

As the conversation drew to a close, I felt there was much more to talk about, but we were out of time. I recalled a small banner with a printed message from His Holiness the Dalai Lama about compassion that I bought many years ago in the temple gift shop. I kept it close by my side when I wrote and wanted to share the message with Venerable. The title of the banner was 'Selfishness' and the message said:

We can also approach the importance of compassion through intelligent reasoning. If I help another person and show concern for him or her, then I myself will benefit from that. However, if I harm others, eventually I will be in trouble. I often joke, half seriously, that if we wish to be truly selfish then we should be wisely selfish rather than foolishly selfish. If we use our intelligence well, we can gain insights as to how we can fulfil our own self-interest by leading a compassionate way of life.

Venerable smiled after I read it to her and said, 'Oh, I remember that banner, you got the last one.'

The Heart of Compassion in Venerable Dhammananda's Words

When people ask me to describe Buddhism in one word, I say the 'heart'. Compassion really begins in our hearts first. The Latin root for the word compassion is *pati*, which means to suffer, and the prefix *com* means with. Compassion originating from *compati* literally means to suffer with. The Buddha's message was very simple. He chose to start with a common human experience, namely suffering. Everyone born into this life will experience the suffering caused by this physical existence. His true message was that all of us can be free from suffering, which is caused by clinging to the self which is not real. This was his enlightenment, and he was known as the Buddha, the fully enlightened One.

When the Buddha sent out the first batch of enlightened monks, he instructed them to share his understanding with people so that they could overcome their suffering. He also gave the monks this important guidance: be of benefit for other people's well-being and happiness. Thus, when a person gains this insight, he or she is no longer acting for themselves only, but also for the benefit of others' well-being and happiness. This is the balance I always keep in mind.

One of the best examples of an individual who was willing to offer himself for the benefit of humankind was Christ. As a student of religion, I studied the Gospel for a year, and was particularly interested in the crucified Christ, how he emptied himself – surrendered himself totally to God. I even had a picture of Christ on the cross above my bed. I really felt strongly that Jesus gave up his life for a greater cause.

During the last day of persecution prior to being arrested by the Romans, Jesus went up on the mountain to meditate. Being human, Jesus was afraid of death and did not want to die, but being committed to God's will, he accepted his death. Even though I am a Buddhist, this message spoke to me of Jesus' pure faith and commitment. He was willing to give up what was most precious to him, namely, his own life, his self.

When Jesus was dying on the cross, he called out to God, 'Oh Father, why have you forsaken me?' This is a deep spiritual yearning to be in touch with reality. The crucified Christ is an important Christian symbol because he represents a total rendering of self to the higher self. Jesus was willing to offer himself for the benefit of others. Speaking as a Buddhist, I truly appreciate what he did. I have a beautiful wood carving of the crucified Christ on the wall in the temple library that a Catholic priest gave me. People often ask me, 'Venerable Mother, why do you have this Christian symbol on your wall?' The image of the crucified Christ on the wall encourages the spirit of total compassion and commitment.

The first thing I did when I decided to receive ordination was take the Bodhisattva's vows in the year 2000. I had read a lot about the Bodhisattva path and understood that embarking on a monastic path really required making a commitment. By taking the vows I confirmed my complete faith in the Buddha as an enlightened person and made a commitment to walk the path of enlightenment. I also undertook the commitment to work on behalf of the well-being of others.

I have an expression – *The heart of the Bodhisattva is ideal for socially engaged Buddhism.* As Buddhists, we talk so much about metta (loving-kindness) and karuna (compassion for another person's suffering). This is the Buddhist practice. When this heart feels compassion this *maha karuna* rises spontaneously, and we have to do something about it.

Buddhist temples can be socially engaged by providing compassionate support to local people during times of crisis. Within the Chinese character for crisis there is also another character, 'opportunity'; thus during times of crisis, we also have an opportunity to help. Buddhist temples frequently have surpluses of food that they can easily share with their local communities. In emergency situations food is needed, medicine is needed, spiritual support is needed, and direction is needed to guide people's lives.

In the spring of 2020, during the initial stages of the coronavirus pandemic, we shared our food with local day labourers who couldn't work because of the pandemic. The first time, we provided food for forty people. We provided each family with 5 kilograms of rice, as well as oil, chili paste, soap, shampoo, instant noodles, milk, drinks, fresh vegetables such as cabbage and pumpkin, and so on. A factory close by contributed eggs and bread. Later, the sangha (lay community members) joined in, and we served one hundred people, increasing to one hundred and fifty and then two hundred. This is truly from heart to heart – a Buddhist practice.

At Songdhammakalyani Temple we practise another form of social engagement; we are an eco-temple. We aim to have zero waste and generate this as an example for other Thai temples to follow. There are a few temples with this awareness, but to be able to deal with the problem of waste effectively, we need to work collectively.

Each one of us in our heart has the potential to help others, but we don't allow our potential to be actualized. We realize this when we think, 'Oh we don't know what to do, what to do.' The Buddha talks about the importance of giving. Start from wherever you are at and do what you can, and there will be other hearts who will join you in this great compassionate work.

CHAPTER 8

Forgiveness

To forgive someone you must love unconditionally.

The conversation I had with Venerable about kindness and compassion led to more questions. What she'd said was all well and good in the abstract, but what happens when you're emotionally triggered? Or like when a dear friend suddenly starts yelling at you in the middle of the parking lot? Compassion was the last thing on my mind as I felt hot anger rising in my belly. *How dare she?* Followed by the unanswered question: *Could I ever forgive her?*

My friend's reaction surprised me and seemed to come out of nowhere. We were on a road trip together. I had never travelled with her before but by day ten we were both strained. I could tell by her cold, silent demeanour at morning coffee that she was growing impatient with me. I asked her what was wrong, but she brushed me off.

Later that day a rear tyre blew out, and we pulled over to assess the situation. Relieved to be off the expressway I muttered under my breath, 'At least we weren't on the freeway.' Apparently, I repeated this out loud one too many times. She began shouting, 'You said that three times! It is no big deal, why are you so stressed? You're making the situation worse.' I froze, startled by her outburst. I tried to talk to her but only aggravated the situation.

Furious, I stomped off to wander the aisles of a nearby drugstore. I was tense all over, my jaw clamped, my breathing shallow, my muscles constricted, and my chest wound tight like a loaded spring. We did not talk all afternoon and that evening we avoided each other as I plotted my revenge: I would book an airplane ticket, leaving her stranded to make the nine-hour drive home alone. I would never speak to her again – all my Buddhist training flew out the window.

When we find ourselves stuck in anger and resentment, what can we do? How do we move from resentment to forgiveness? Could I forgive my friend for the hurt I felt? The answer was no, I was not ready to forgive, my anger was still palpable. I explained the situation to Venerable Dhammananda and asked for her advice. 'I have heard you say that to forgive someone you must love unconditionally. Can you speak about that?'

Venerable Dhammananda said, 'Loving unconditionally means caring for others, even the people we do not like. I remember offering training to the Cambodian *donchees* for three months; they are like the Thai mae chi, laywomen who take the eight precepts, and live in a temple. In 2001, they invited me to come to Cambodia.

'They had suffered so much in the late 1970s because of the brutal regime of the dictator Pol Pot. Between the five women, they had lost a son, a father, a husband, and other members of their family. One donchee told me the story about how the Khmer Rouge murdered monks and drove them into exile. They used the main temple to kill people, they lined them up and shot them. The temples were later deserted.

'The donchees were responsible for reviving Buddhism in Cambodia in 1979 and the first to return to the abandoned temples after the war. They described a horrific scene. 'We had to clean up the bloodstained walls', they said. After some time, the monks returned to the temples and the donchees had to cook for them. Once again, the hierarchical structure of the temple returned despite the fact that the women were there first. I encouraged them to write down their stories, but they didn't, so I am the voice for their history.

'At the end of our time together, I asked them if they could forgive Pol Pot. They said no. Their sense of loss and betrayal was so great that even with all their Buddhist practice they could not overcome their sense of hatred for this man.

'When you offer forgiveness, you let go of your hatred towards the person or people who have hurt you. This hatred is deep rooted, so letting go of it is easier said than done. Each time we remind ourselves of the situation, we relive it, over and over again. Our tension mounts, our hearts beat faster, our muscles clench, and our blood pressure rises. The person who has harmed you has moved on. Who are you hurting now? Only yourself.'

Her tone shifted. 'Actually, overcoming hatred is forgiving *yourself*, because as long as you hold on to the trauma, you will suffer. Most of us will never experience atrocities like the Cambodian women suffered at the hands of Pol Pot, but each one of us has had to cope with painful life experiences. The important question is: how do we deal with the difficult situation?

'You know we always project outward, looking at other people's mistakes, criticizing them, disliking them, blaming them. But if we look inward, we see that we do the same stupid things. Why are we always looking at others? We start by forgiving ourselves for our own shortcomings. When we have loving-kindness for ourselves, we can also forgive others. It goes both ways.'

Dhammananda looked up and said, 'You know Cindy, it is easier to see other people's mistakes than it is our own. Physically we cannot see ourselves. We only see ourselves through the reflection of a mirror. But we can see others directly. I can look at Cindy directly. I can criticize, "Oh Cindy, you could do this better... you look better in that colour." But when I look at myself, I can only see my reflection. Isn't that interesting?'

She went on to explain, 'First of all, we need to concentrate on our own faults to improve ourselves. Forgiving becomes easier when we accept our own imperfections. So, when you are annoyed with someone or angry, look inward. Like that. Be honest with yourself. Then this forgiving becomes easier.'

Venerable spoke with assurance: 'When asking for forgiveness comes truly from our heart, we ease our suffering. Unless you develop this practice of letting go on a personal level you will not be able to free up your heart from suffering.'

I understood what she was saying but knew I was not ready to forgive my friend. Stuck in anger and resentment, I shared my dilemma with Venerable. 'My friend hurt me very deeply. I am still angry and can't find it in my heart to forgive her. What does the Buddha have to say about anger?'

Venerable Dhammananda laughed. 'You know, that happens to all of us, even to the great teachers – whether they want to admit it or not. I get angry but catch myself most of the time. It depends on our practice. If we have been practising well, we can recognize our anger before we express it. The mind reacts so quickly, beyond our ability to control it.

'When someone says something that I do not agree with, I get angry. *How can you be like that, you're so stupid* – I have those thoughts. I criticize them. I am the abbess, more senior and older, and when I get angry, it makes the situation worse. The Buddha does not want us to be angry; he even said if you get angry with the person who got angry – then you are worse off.'

I appreciated Dhammananda's honesty. I had not seen her angry very often but when she was, she could be demanding. One time at the monastery during evening chanting when all the nuns gathered, she clapped her hands and spoke in a loud voice reprimanding us in Thai. I was stunned, probably because I was not used to seeing her behave this way.

Venerable Dhammananda continued the conversation. 'When I am really angry, I take a deep breath and walk in the garden back and forth to exhaust my negative energy before I return to deal with the problem.'

Then she shared that the bigger challenge for her was patience. 'You know, Cindy, I am laughing because I can be very impatient. I am quick at doing things, above average, so being patient with others in my community is a big practice for me. I speak very directly, do not beat about the bush. I am too old for that. Sometimes it is hurtful to the other person. Particularly for Thai people because they are not accustomed to that.'

She looked pensive. 'Sometimes my intention is so strong, I lose my sense of compassion. The root of my impatience is that I want things to go my way. I am coming from a very self-centred place.

'My sangha understands this and that is why they tolerate me. "Oh, Venerable Mother is going through this passage of practising." They are kind to me and endure my impatience.'

I followed what she was saying but circled back to the topic of anger. I asked her how to deal with my anger when I was really upset.

She shifted in her seat, thought for a moment, and then suggested three helpful tips to cope with anger:

First, pause. Take a deep breath.
Second, anchor within yourself.
Third, try to understand the person from their point of view
to see where they stand.

I understood the first two suggestions but struggled with number three. It was hard for me to pause and breathe – much less listen or appreciate the other person when I was emotionally triggered. I realized the bigger question was how to cope with strong emotions.

Dhammananda explained that meditation can help. 'The more we practise, the more we train ourselves to be aware of our thoughts and feelings; and the more we begin to recognize our patterns, the easier it becomes to observe rather than react in the moment.

'We have to be very careful to understand how anger works. As the thought arises, we must watch ourselves – not others, but ourselves. What I usually do is take a deep breath and try to understand the other person's point of view. Then you can have a conversation. But if you do not listen, or give them space, you blow up. I do.'

Venerable Dhammananda looked thoughtful. 'When you are full of anger, full of negativity, your wisdom is clouded, and you do not have time to reflect on the situation. Calm down, pause, and take a deep breath. You can channel the energy in another direction. Ask yourself if you have ever been in a similar situation and done the same thing. We all make mistakes, and we all get angry, but look at it from another angle: can you have compassion for the person who is angry with you?'

Her face softened. 'Once we realize the other person's response is only human, we begin the process of forgiveness. That is why meditation practice is important. As the angry thought arises, take a deep breath, come back to yourself, and catch it before you lose control. When you reflect on the situation, that is when wisdom comes.'

The next thing she said took me by surprise. 'When something like this happens, when you are sure you are right, that is your pride talking – you are still thirty per cent responsible. Very often when I get annoyed, I say something that is too strong. I have to take responsibility for my part in the situation.'

I had never even considered my part in the interaction with my friend. Clearly, I said something to upset her, or she would not have reacted so strongly. I was stuck in the 'blame game' and thinking out of selfish pride that I was right and she was wrong. I realized that even though I was not the one who started the argument, my worrisome comments had played a part. Also, by perpetuating my anger I was hanging on to resentment and not helping the situation.

Although I apologized to my friend right after the initial blow-up happened and we drove home together, our feud continued for several months. I had not made the commitment deep in my heart to forgive her – until one day out of the blue she called to apologize. Ironically, it was my friend and not me who showed unconditional love. She told me how much she loved me and how much our friendship meant to her – that really touched me. We began talking again and eventually healed the rift between us.

I reflected on my conversation with Venerable Dhammananda about anger and forgiveness. One thing I know, for sure: I will probably lose it again at some point, but at least I can think about pausing and taking a deep breath. Also, when anger happens, like Venerable said, I can forgive myself. I am not perfect and never will be, but can learn from my mistakes and continue to move forward.

Practising Forgiveness in Venerable Dhammananda's Words

Opening our hearts to love others unconditionally is what leads us on the path to forgiveness. A mother's love is a good example of unconditional love. A mother can forgive her children no matter what they have done. Other people may judge her children for their mistakes, but a mother's love remains constant. The real question is: can you really love your enemies the way you love your children? That is the true meaning of loving-kindness.

Loving unconditionally starts by learning to forgive ourselves. So many people have difficulty forgiving themselves. How do you learn to love yourself? This is not easy. We can learn to practise loving-kindness towards ourselves by focusing inward and mindfully examining our own behaviour. For example, if another person is being criticized, we notice it, but we are not upset. But if someone criticizes us, our anger rises and before we know it we react – we automatically want to get back at them. But just stop for a minute, look at yourself and ask, 'Have I ever made the same mistake?'

When we start to look at the situation from this angle, we begin to relax. Just like a mother loves her child, we release our judgements – it's only natural that things happen like this. With this understanding comes acceptance, and once we learn to accept ourselves, we are already in the process of forgiving. Once we learn to forgive ourselves, forgiving others becomes much easier.

Anger is a particularly challenging emotion for most of us to forgive, but meditation practice can help us learn to cope. 'The practice of mindfulness can be compared to looking at life through a magnifying glass, things are enlarged, and we can see each part in minute detail, rising and falling away. Without the practice of meditation, we do not realize that this is the way everything happens; it rises and falls away.

'Similarly, when our ears hear insulting words, a message is sent to our mind, and without the control of mindfulness, the mind immediately sends a message to our body, and before we even realize it, we have kicked the person we felt had insulted us! It just happened. But with our training in meditation, we realize that things don't just happen; it follows from A to B to C to D, not from A to D. Each step affects the next. With meditation practice we observe our mind, we are aware of how transitory our emotions are. If we feel angry, we watch the anger, "so this is what anger is like", we observe. When anger arises, we feel hot and bothered, we feel its heat and understand how the mind can affect the body. We have all heard that people with a quick temper can blow up. But with the practice of meditation, we learn to watch ourselves very carefully and catch the anger before it affects our body. We say to the anger, "Oh, there you are, I recognize you", and it disappears by itself.'[33]

Anger and hatred can be very deep rooted, like when you grow a plant. By watering the seeds of hatred, we are nurturing the plant to grow into a very large tree, which not only affects you, it affects other people. I have an example of this from my own life. Thai people of my generation were brought up to believe that the Burmese are our unforgivable enemies. Throughout Thai history there have been many wars with the Burmese when they came in and attacked us, burning and destroying property, desecrating Buddha statues. We told ourselves stories about the Burmese. If we heard loud noises in the house, we would say, 'You scared me, I thought the Burmese were coming to get us.' We were brought up to hate, refuse, and deny the Burmese. Therefore, many of us, like my sister, refused to go to Myanmar.

The very first thing I did after I was ordained was travel to Myanmar to visit Shwedagon, the magnificent stupa. I went there to bow to the Buddha and experience the sacred energy at this site. I acknowledged that whatever stories I had learned about the Burmese – truthful or not – I forgave them. I also asked for their forgiveness because I did not know how my own hatred may have harmed them in the past.

When countries are fighting, you don't know who is cutting off whose head. So, we ask for forgiveness for the harm we may have done. This is a very important message to understand: that in the process of practising forgiveness you are healing yourself and making yourself whole again.

When living in a community, inevitably conflict happens. If we are willing to examine our behaviour and acknowledge our share in causing the conflict, we can learn to live harmoniously with others. We acknowledge that we may have done something wrong or said something hurtful to the other person. Once we take responsibility for our behaviour, we can go to the other person, admit when we make a mistake and ask for forgiveness. By doing this, we start to generate genuine loving-kindness and compassion towards others, and this loving-kindness is the basis for creating harmonious communities.

CHAPTER 9

Jealousy

It eats you up from the inside.

Following our discussion about anger and forgiveness, Venerable moved on to another difficult topic, jealousy. The subject came up when a friend of mine, Lauren, was a guest on Casual Buddhism. She spoke with Venerable Dhammananda about the pressure she felt to advance in her career and how she suffered when she saw someone at work promoted ahead of her.

Venerable Dhammananda said, 'It is always good to be striving forward in your career, but when someone is given a promotion, how come we feel so unhappy? Is that jealousy? Remember, in the four limbs of the Brahma Vihara, the third one, mudita (joy in another person's success), is one of the most difficult because it is a deep practice of overcoming oneself. The Buddha makes a key point of helping us let go of our attachment to ourselves. When it is our own promotion, we are thrilled, but when it is someone else's, we become resentful of their success.'

Lauren asked Venerable, 'How do I practise mudita?'

'It is not easy to accept another person's success. More than accept it, you have to feel joyful for them. There is much clinging to I, me, mine. If I am only happy when the promotion happens to me, then in that case my happiness is very small. Try a new way of looking at things: when you hear other people's good news, practise feeling happy for them.'

Venerable Dhammananda spoke with assurance, 'My advice is to be yourself. Do your best work without concern for the result. You may not get the promotion this time, but if you continue to do good work, a positive result will follow. The good karma you perform is never lost. You will reap the reward at some point. And once we begin to understand this, we calm down.

'Lauren, when you do your best, you see your potential to flourish, like a flower blossoming. You know, when the flower blooms we feel happy. Think of that flower blossoming when you see another person getting promoted and you will feel joyful inside.'

Venerable Dhammananda's voice softened. 'Be kind to yourself. Even when the outcome is not what you wanted, thank yourself for all you have accomplished. Give yourself credit. Prioritize the love you have for yourself, and this will reduce your stress. Practise much healing and kindness to yourself.'

With a look of concern, she added, 'It is not easy living in this world. I went through something similar when I was working at the university, but in looking back, I realized there were more important things in life than work, especially my relationship to my family. I had three boys and felt I did not spend as much time with them as I would have liked. I regret that now. I was struggling so hard to prove to the world and myself that I was a success. What I sacrificed... was it worth it? I think it may not have been the best decision. What's important is your connection to your husband, your family. We tend to focus so much on our personal success that we forget about our important connections to others.'

Venerable Dhammananda lightened up and said, 'I hope sharing my experience is helpful. Lauren, you are a really good person. If I were your boss, I would be very happy to have you working for me because you are someone who works hard and wants to do their best.'

Lauren smiled. 'Thank you, Venerable. What beautiful reflections. I was really struck by the idea that we do not control outcomes; it helps me to relax. Like you said, I can do my best, but I do not control the results. I also like what you said about how my happiness will be small if I only focus on my own success. If I can expand that, my happiness grows exponentially.'

Venerable Dhammananda beamed. 'Your face looks softer now. Although this is the first time I've met you, I can see a change between Lauren when we started and Lauren now. I can see you ease up like a flower blossoming... beautiful. I feel such happiness inside.'

Practising Mudita in Venerable Dhammananda's Words

The four brahmaviharas are metta or loving-kindness, karuna or compassion, mudita or joy, and upekkha or equanimity. The third of these qualities, mudita, is joy in another person's success. This joy for others starts with loving-kindness. Thai people often end our meditations by wishing all sentient beings loving-kindness. That's all well and good, but do we really mean it?

To be authentic we must practise loving-kindness for all sentient beings, including our enemies. To really spread loving-kindness, it must go out to everyone, not just the people we love. Think of the face of the person you hate: can you share your love for that person? Let's be honest, imagine the person who has hurt you for so many years: can we forgive him or her for that? This joy for others starts with loving-kindness. True loving-kindness for others is a deep-rooted practice that develops gradually in our minds over time, not overnight.

Let me give you an example. One day at the temple we were creating a mud house. Since I am elderly, I was asked to do the lighter work of chopping the clay. We put the chunk of clay in the water to soak and soften overnight. The next day I noticed that the clay I was chopping disintegrated into finer particles – minerals of the earth. In that second, I suddenly realized that I was the clay. I felt that connection with myself and what I was holding onto.

In Buddhism we talk about the four elements – earth, water, fire, and air. We are made up of the composition of these four elements. By this I mean that we simply borrow these elements that become our bodies (selves) and, after some time, all of us must return what we have borrowed to the greater universe. Supposedly I call myself Dhammananda, and you Cindy, but eventually I will return to the earth as one of the four elements.

So, working with the clay I felt an immediate connection between the clay and myself. With this sudden realization, I let go of I, me, my, mine, and, along with that, I let go of some anger I had been carrying towards another person. I let go of judging him as the bad culprit, and thinking I am the better person. The barrier between me and him suddenly fell away.

I think this ability to let go stems from our practice, which allows us to understand the Truth – the Truth, with a capital T, which is very much the core teaching of the Buddha. When we sense this deeper connection, we can really let go of that burning hatred inside. We become less judgemental and more forgiving of the other person.

Once we begin to understand the true nature of our essential selves, we can begin to let go of resentment and hatred – that barrier of separation with others. We allow ourselves to generate loving-kindness towards others, and to feel mudita – joy in another person's success.

CHAPTER 10

Despair

The Bodhisattva's heart is not limited.

Nancy, another guest on Casual Buddhism, felt the enormity of the world's problems weighing on her and was discouraged. She began her conversation with Venerable Dhammananda with a question: 'In these troubled times there's so much suffering and despair, violence and greed – what are some of the teachings of the Buddha that help us to maintain our faith, our hope?'

Venerable Dhammananda paused for a moment and then said, 'Hope happens when we open our hearts and let others in. I think particularly now, people suffer from depression. They are overwhelmed – worried about work and family and the larger problems of the world. When we are depressed, we become fearful and withdrawn. Our focus turns inward. We think about receiving rather than giving. When we change our mindset and think about giving to others, we feel better.'

She folded her hands on the desk. 'Let me give an example. When the pandemic happened, the whole country went into lockdown. You know no one had ever experienced this in their lifetime, not me, nor my mother, nor my grandmother. We had to buy rice for our kitchen, but I was thinking of the poor outside who live on a daily wage and suddenly there was no work. How were they going to eat? Some of them gathered mushrooms from the forest – that was how poor they were, they had no food for the next day.

'We came up with a plan to share our rice with them. We went to the market and bought two sacks of rice, which is about 100 kilos. We divided that into smaller sacks of 2 kilos each so we could give it to more people. There was a photo of me handing out rice that was put on Facebook, and it went viral. This one man sitting in his house, very comfortable, said he could not stand to see an old nun doing this and thought, "I must do something." And do you know what that man did? The next week, he drove in with 600 kilos of rice. Instead of having us scoop it into small bags he had already packaged the rice into 5-kilo bags. This man gave us more than 10,000 kilos of rice for distribution. Can you imagine? This all started from us giving 2 kilos of rice and expanded into this huge amount.'

Venerable Dhammananda pictured in April of 2020 distributing food to the local people in the initial year of the COVID pandemic

Venerable Dhammananda said, 'Do you see? Don't think you cannot do anything, start with what you have by doing small things. Each one of us, in our heart, has the potential to help, but we do not act on that.

'If you feel discouraged, ask yourself what can you do? You are just one small woman, doing a small amount, everything is limited. But the Bodhisattva's heart is not limited. When you start to do something, other like-minded people will join you in this great work. Always believe in that. Always believe we have the potential to connect to the larger energy to make things happen.'

Nancy asked Venerable Dhammananda, 'What is the best way to cultivate those seeds of connection?'

'Just speak. Express yourself. Maybe you will make the decision not to air your negative feelings on social media from now on. Whatever means you have, send out wholesome energy. And if Cindy starts from her corner of the world, then Nancy starts from her corner of the world, we gather all this good energy of people with wholesome hearts – wholesome expression (in Pali it is called *kusala*) – and together, this energy will blossom. We must believe this, and that is the hope for the future of our world.'

Looking thoughtful for a moment, Venerable added, 'You know, the successful projects in the world always start with a small number of people who share the same kind heart and that is how we move forward to reach the larger community.'

Nancy, still questioning herself, said, 'Sometimes I am so discouraged I get stuck. What happens when I am unable to move forward?'

Venerable Dhammananda was undeterred. 'You have to go back to the basics of the wholesome mind. Instead of allowing the negative mindset to arise, focus on the positive.'

'But how?' Nancy asked.

'We can change the energy of our mind. Most of the time we are preoccupied with our own thoughts and not really present. This coming back to the present involves letting go of I, me, mine, and giving our full attention to the other. You could say it is kind of a distraction, to shift our perspective onto someone else. I freely admit this is easier said than done.'

Venerable Dhammananda offered an example. 'If you have a friend who is scared because she does not want to be alone, you could go stay with her. You are giving her a sense of safety. We feel better when we help others. This is the Bodhisattva's heart; we feel compassion and our hearts let the compassion flow.'

Nancy nodded and smiled. Her face relaxed and she shared her thoughts. 'Helping others is such an important part of who we are. Sometimes I feel too afraid or vulnerable to open up and create that space for myself and others. We are all a work in progress. Right now, I have the feeling I want to do more. I may be limited in what I can do, but I can accept whatever is present and stay open to possibilities. I can stay open to opportunities and continue to create that spaciousness in my heart.'

Venerable Dhammananda's Teaching on Despair

I have a saying about suffering. Think of suffering
– you suffer. Limit your thinking and suffering has
no hold. This is also a way of saying once you are in
emotional pain, if all you do is think about the pain you
get stuck there and it doesn't improve. You can't get out
of it – it's like a cycle that keeps repeating. When we are
struggling with a difficult emotion it is sometimes hard
to let go.

If you have had a particularly hurtful experience, you
push it down and bury it below the surface of your
conscious mind. The repressed feeling can sometimes
resurface when you are in deep meditation. When a
difficult emotion arises, you feel the pain just like when
you first experienced it. You ask: how can I deal with
this; how can I let go? If your state of mind is deeply
anchored in vipassana – when your mind is strong
enough – you can see things as they are.

You may have been avoiding this painful experience
for thirty to forty years. But now with Buddha mind,
you are in the space to say, 'This bad experience could
be anyone's experience; it doesn't necessarily have to be
mine.' When you look at it with Buddha mind, you see
it very clearly.

Unless and until your mind is deeply settled in this Buddha nature, letting go isn't possible. You need to have this deep concentration and get to the level of insight meditation, where you are wearing this cloak of the Buddha. When you are blessed with the radiance of Buddhahood, you can look at it head on. Then you can let go of the experience and it will not disturb you anymore.

This is not easy. But I have lived with this type of experience, one which has been buried for forty years. When we understand the true nature of the experience, we can let it let go. It's very much about the central meaning of Buddhism to see things as they are.

When you reach the level of vipassana meditation, that mental training will allow you to face what has been trapped inside you for so many years. Suddenly, you realize, 'I don't have to suffer; this experience doesn't even have to be mine.' You have carried that feeling of hurt for a long time. We are so attached to our experiences. When we stop clinging to our experience, we can really let go and be free of suffering.

CHAPTER 11

Loneliness

Come back to this fresh existence.

During a conversation related to the theme of despair, I spoke to Venerable Dhammananda about how lonely I felt after I divorced my husband. We had been married for thirty-three years. Living on my own, I missed my former partner and companion – and my heart was broken. I felt untethered and disconnected – uncomfortable in my own skin. All I wanted to do was run away to escape from my misery. I fought my feelings and got stuck in the expectation that I 'should' be happy – as if I were not supposed to feel sad, as if something were wrong with me.

On top of that, it was the second year of the COVID-19 pandemic, and living by myself while being quarantined was really getting to me. There were times I did not see people for days. Thankfully, I had a hiking group that met in the early morning. We wore masks and walked six feet apart. Being out in nature helped, but I really missed spending time with friends.

I was not the only one struggling with loneliness – everyone was longing for more connection – and I turned to Venerable Dhammananda for advice. I wondered what the Buddha had to say about loneliness and asked Venerable Dhammananda if it was a natural part of human suffering or my own self-preoccupation.

Venerable Dhammananda replied that, in fact, 'We *all* are alone from the beginning. When we are born, we come into this world alone with our own karma, independent in the sense that we are not connected to anyone, even our loved ones.'

I heard what Venerable Dhammananda was saying but fought a nagging feeling that made me want to delve deeper into the topic. I was curious if Venerable Dhammananda had ever struggled with loneliness and asked, 'Was there ever a time in your life when you felt lonely? Maybe as abbess of the temple?'

Venerable Dhammananda responded that, as a monastic, she did not suffer from loneliness, but there was a time in her lay life when she did feel terribly alone. She told me her story.

'In 1981, when I was thirty-seven, I went through a very difficult time that lasted about six months. I felt very sad, even though I had three sons and was still married to my husband. I could hardly eat and when I did, I was just going through the motions, not realizing what I was tasting.

'My life was completely meaningless. Even though I had a family and a successful academic career, I felt worthless and empty inside. On weekends, I would meditate with my mother, hidden in the back of the third floor of the main temple, crying. I felt something was wrong. Being a wife, mother, and professor was not enough anymore.

'I retreated into a back room and started to draw simple line sketches. My boys would sneak in and quietly peer over my shoulder. They were concerned because I was not playing with them.

'"What are you doing?" they asked.

'"Drawing."

'They liked what I was doing and often came to watch me. Then, my husband came and asked me what I was doing. Again, I explained, and he said, "Good. You should write an explanation of what each drawing means to you."

'That collection of sketches became a kind of philosophy of life. On one page was a drawing and on the opposite page was an explanation of what the drawing meant. I had so much material it turned into a book. I published that book and it rose to the top ten. It was reprinted many times. When you are lonely, if you have something productive to do that nourishes you, it helps you come through your crisis.

'Eventually, I happened to talk to a psychiatrist in New York who listened to my story, and he said, "Oh, you're so lucky you came through your midlife crisis by yourself." That is when I realized I'd had a midlife crisis. I did not know what to call it until then.'

Venerable Dhammananda said definitively, 'Yes. That is right, "loneliness" was the key word. Drawing was a more worldly way of solving the problem. But when you get into meditation, this coming back to your breathing, this mindfulness, really helps.

'When we are stuck in the trenches of our loneliness, sitting or walking meditation can help as well – our thinking mind is so busy with stress and worry, it is hard to pay attention to our surroundings. We need to shift our mental focus to come back to the present moment. When you practise mindfulness, your mind is fully focused in the here and now, and loneliness disappears. Come back to yourself, your breath. It really helps not to be preoccupied with one hundred and one things but come back to this fresh existence.'

I shared with Venerable Dhammananda that I really liked the concept 'fresh existence', but also realized that when I am anxious it is hard for me to meditate. Sundays, I told her, are hardest for me. That is the day when I think about family and being together. A dull ache sets in that is physically painful.

She said, 'Loneliness eats you up from the inside, it is like walking without your spirit. When that happens, go for a walk, get outdoors.' She suggested that doing something creative could also help: 'Immerse yourself in a project like painting, handicrafts, or listening to music – anything to quiet the turmoil in your mind.'

After we spoke, I thought about our conversation and realized there are times when I am comfortable being alone. I had an 'aha' moment. I remembered a time seven months after my divorce when I was visiting Mendocino, a remote seaside town along California's Pacific Coast. As I sat on a bench overlooking the magnificent Pacific Ocean, mesmerized by the vast expanse of water, I felt as if I were floating in the undulating waves, drifting in and out. I was serene and peaceful for the first time in months, and comfortable being alone. There was a feeling of joy in wholeness. It takes courage to cross the wide abyss of our loneliness, but once we do, we humbly open our hearts and unlock the doors that have kept us separate for so long: we *return to this fresh existence.*

Venerable Dhammananda's Teaching on Loneliness

Our true nature from the very beginning is that we are born alone with our karma. We are who we are because we are the collective result of our own past karma. This does not mean that Buddhism is fatalistic. Buddhism talks about how the future depends very much on our own decision making in the present moment. When we begin to accept this, we become more comfortable with the idea of being alone.

Let me explain the notion of karma and what it means. Karma is action with intention. Suppose we are talking about a glass of water. Half of the glass is not very clean, but you decide to put clean water in it. We are the one who is deciding what kind of water to put in this glass; therefore, we are determining our own life. Making the decision happens now, so that the future karma – our future action – will be directed accordingly.

When it comes to having choice, part of who we are depends upon previous actions that happened in previous births. We did not choose our parents in this lifetime. This happened because of our previous karma. But once we are born, from then on, it is our own decision, our own mental formation that determines our future direction. With this understanding, we realize that it's important to live mindfully in this present moment. We can do this by tuning into our present surroundings and paying attention to our breath.

When we practise mindfulness, our minds are redirected to the present time. The experience of loneliness is just the opposite. Our thinking mind is so preoccupied with worry and doubt that it's hard to sense where we're at. This is why, when we are feeling lonely, I recommend coming back to our breath. Come back to yourself, your breathing, and your mood shifts.

The feeling of loneliness comes with the thought process which takes us very far away. We get caught up in thinking about the past or worrying about the future. If, for example, we stop thinking for a second and come back to the simple sensation of our fingers touching one another, things become much simpler. Come back and just observe your feeling. This is one way to change your perspective and allow yourself to reconnect with your present surroundings. Our loneliness begins to dissipate when we come back to the present moment. The practice is simple, we simply need to let ourselves be.

CHAPTER 12

Craving

Always craving causes more suffering.

Craving in Venerable Dhammananda's Words

We live in a consumer culture, which exacerbates our craving. We are bombarded daily with commercials on our phones and TVs, luring us to buy one more thing until it becomes an obsession. For example, you may have a closet full of shoes, but you think you need one more pair to match a certain outfit. Gradually, your closet fills up with clothing you hardly ever wear. Having more does not necessarily mean you will be happy; you may be unhappy because you are never satisfied. Living in a state of constant desire leads to craving. On the other hand, a person with only three sets of clothing may feel she has enough. Her happiness doesn't depend on external possessions.

There's a story in Thai Buddhist folklore about hungry ghosts, known as *pret*. Pret are ghosts with only a tiny opening for a mouth so that they live in a state of perpetual hunger. These spirits are said to have been stingy and greedy in a previous life. At some of our festivals people make white noodles, like thin spaghetti, so that the ghosts can suck it in through their mouths. Thais offer this noodle, khanom cheen, on special occasions because we never know whether one of our ancestors might be a hungry ghost, and we want to make sure they don't suffer.

A popular Thai story about a hungry ghost features one of the Buddha's main disciples, Venerable Sariputra. The Buddha had two main disciples, one who sat on his left, Sariputra, and the other, Maudgalyayana, who sat on his right. Sariputra was known for his wisdom and Maudgalyayana for his miracles. One night, Sariputra's mother from a previous lifetime came to the door of his temple wanting to see him. She looked like a skeleton with straggly hair and was dressed in rags. The monk who greeted her refused to let her in. When the monk described the woman to Sariputra, he confirmed that she was his mother. Venerable Maudgalyayana heard about this story and went to make an offering of food on her behalf. Performing this ritual act is called 'making merit', and in this case Venerable Maudgalyayana dedicated his merit to the hungry ghost who was Sariputra's mother. The next time Sariputra's mother appeared at the residence, she was well dressed and appeared to be well fed. Through receiving Venerable Maudgalyayana's offering, she had been able to let go of her greed.

There are several lessons to glean from this story. When we are in a constant state of craving, we are like the hungry ghost, and this causes suffering. Our greed keeps expanding along with our desire. We are consumed by our own selfish needs and never satisfied. If we practise acceptance that what we have is enough, there is no need to acquire more. Right now, we are okay. Possessing that state of mind presents an opportunity for divine existence.

CHAPTER 13

Grasping

All the suffering and problems that we have are
nothing but the clinging on to I, me, my, mine.

In January of 2020 I visited the temple, shortly before my first book – a memoir called *Finding Venerable Mother* – was published. I had given Venerable Dhammananda an advance reader's copy to review and was anxiously awaiting her feedback. I was not convinced she would like it, given the whole idea of memoir – writing about oneself – is so self-involved. This focus on the personal narrative ran counter to Buddhism which involves letting go of the ego and grasping. Even so, I hoped for the best and wanted her praise above all else.

It was mid-afternoon, and we had planned to meet at 3 p.m. in her favourite spot, a shaded area located underneath the dormitory, protected by a roof overhead. I sat and waited at a small, stone table. The air was still and hot. I glanced down at my watch, 3.05 p.m.; the waiting was excruciating.

Within minutes she drove up on the maroon scooter she now uses as she gets older, comfortably perched as she pulled into her familiar parking space alongside the table. As she stepped off the bike, she carried a copy of my book in her hand. I took a deep breath as she began the conversation. 'So, I have read your book. There are a few changes I want to make. You use the word "pray" a lot, but in Buddhism we do not pray, we chant. Like here', she pointed to a page, 'This passage should read, "We pressed our palms together, bowed, and knelt as the nuns chanted a blessing" – rather than prayed – "for us."'

I was searching for signs of reaction in her face, but her expression remained neutral. *What is she thinking? Does she like the book?* She continued flipping through the pages showing me where she had marked other changes.

This had not been a particularly easy visit. I sensed Venerable was frustrated with me, but I was not sure why. Then, looking directly at me, she said, 'You remember the three brothers, greed, anger, and delusion? We are talking about grasping. Grasping for I, me, my, mine. You say *my* Venerable Mother, *my* teacher – this is grasping. When you let go of this grasping, bodhicitta – enlightened mind – can blossom.'

I was shocked and hurt by her response. I thought I had written a beautiful tribute to her, and she saw it as an example of my possessiveness. After our conversation I spent a quiet afternoon, feeling miserable. Later that evening, all the nuns gathered as usual for chanting. Venerable Dhammananda often gave a dharma talk afterwards.

Tired after a long day, my shoulders sagged. Venerable Dhammananda began her dharma talk in Thai and then translated it into English. As she launched into the English version, something very powerful happened. My whole body tingled. I felt an energetic surge shoot through me, and all my senses jolted awake. I perked up and sat forward, fully aware I was receiving her transmission and the story was meant for me.

The story Dhammananda shared was about a nun who realized she was pregnant. The Buddha understood that this woman had been married before and probably had not realized she was pregnant until she was already ordained. The question was whether she could remain in robes, but rather than make the decision himself, the Buddha wanted the community – the sangha – to decide. The sangha questioned the woman about the last time she had relations with her husband and determined it was prior to receiving ordination. They decided the woman would be allowed to remain ordained, keep her son for one year, and then relinquish the child for adoption.

The essence of the story was that the mother could not stop grieving for her son and wanted to spend time with him. She finally saw him again at the age of twenty-one. He was also ordained and was very harsh with her. The mother felt bad, but she was unable to stop clinging to him. Eventually the woman was able to stop clinging, let go of her craving, and became enlightened. That was Venerable Dhammananda's message to me.

I was so energized I could not sleep that night. I understood what she was telling me. She felt I was too possessive of her, *my* Venerable Dhammananda, clinging to her and idolizing her in a way that was unhealthy. She was sending me a message to let go of my attachment to her and allow for a spaciousness to grow in our relationship.

The next day we met again, and I decided to bring up the subject of grasping. She drove up on her motor scooter and parked. Once she had a chance to get settled, I asked her directly, 'Yesterday you were saying I am grasping at you? Do you feel that way?'

'Yes. I feel that when I read your book.'

'Do you think I am placing you on a pedestal?'

'Maybe. On the positive side you were saying "Venerable Mother" helped you heal your suffering. But when you go overboard people might feel like that "Oh, she is *my* teacher, *my* venerable mother"; it's too much. You need to tone it down, so people get that the learning is not personal, but universal.'

I took a deep breath and processed what she was saying. 'So, are you telling me I need to let go of grasping to allow my mind to be enlightened?'

'Yes', she said. 'When you hold onto something so tight', she gripped a water bottle to demonstrate, 'it is not comfortable. When you simply touch it, then it feels natural. Allow freedom of the other party.'

I was beginning to understand what she was saying. For years, I tried to control our relationship by constantly seeking her approval. I was grateful when she showed me attention but was also jealous when she singled out others for praise. My possessiveness was a kind of adulation, but I was suffocating her, although that was not my intention.

I wanted more clarification, so I asked, 'I needed to have faith in you to learn, but somewhere I crossed a line between faith and adoration. Can you explain this to me?'

'Yes. Adoration is like, whatever the teacher says is good, without coming back to question what is right. You must have that righteousness within you. Sometimes your teacher is not right. You must be able to tell her kindly, protectively, when she is wrong. In the Vinaya, it says that if the teacher does wrong, the disciple must protect him. My responsibility as your teacher is to guide you as my disciple, to educate and support you. The support works both ways. You must have your own sense of righteousness and tell me when I am wrong.'

She grinned and added, 'There are things you may do better than your teacher, right?'

I thought about this conversation for months afterwards, and it took a long time for me to fully process the depth of what she was saying. Although her initial response to the book felt hurtful, eventually I understood she was encouraging me to let go of my craving – my attachment to her. She wanted me to take her off the pedestal and think for myself. Also, and more importantly, she wanted me to let go of clinging to her so I would have the freedom to grow spiritually.

Three years later, as I was writing this book, I thought about how, in all the years I have known Venerable, she keeps coming back to one theme: *Letting go of I, me, my, mine*. I asked her why this was so important to her.

She leaned forward with a look of earnest concern and said, 'That is the core message of the Buddha. All the suffering and problems that we have are nothing but the clinging on to I, me, my, mine. If we want to experience true freedom, we need to be able to let go of the self, which from the very beginning is not there.'

And without prompting from me, she brought up our conversation from three years earlier and said, 'And there was a time you were clinging to me as your teacher. You had so much faith in me, but I felt it was too much. I was afraid I would hurt your feelings by telling you.'

I was surprised to hear this and reassured her I appreciated her feedback. Her honesty had helped me look at our relationship and where and how I needed to let go. If she had not challenged me in the way she did that day, I would have remained stuck in unhealthy behaviours. She helped me to understand a core Buddhist teaching: clinging to oneself causes suffering. I am forever grateful.

Anatta or No Self in Venerable Dhammananda's Words

Non-self or no self is a key concept of Buddhism. *Anatta* is from Pali. *An + atta. An* is a negative prefix, and *atta* means 'self', so generally we translate this to mean no self. The theory of *anatta* is unique to the Buddha's teaching. To understand his teaching, I need to provide you with the historical background of religious beliefs that existed under Brahmanism, which preceded Buddhism. The Buddha's discovery of the new theory of non-self evolved from the definition in Brahmanism but differed significantly from the earlier Hindu teachings.

We need to understand that during the time of Brahmanism in India there was a belief in the concept of self, which is known in Sanskrit as *atman*. Atman is a self, this self is a small 's', that is, each one of us sitting here is an individual self. The characteristic of this self, this atman, is unchanging, eternal. We move on from one birth to another with exactly the same self, taking on only the new form. It is the very same atman that goes from one life to another. It is like we change into a new shirt everyday but the person wearing it is the same.

Then there is God, the supreme being which is called paramatman. Param means the great or supreme, and atman, in this context, refers to the Self with a capital 'S', which is the Supreme being or Brahman, the Universal Self. Paramatman is also eternal and changeless. When you become enlightened you achieve moksha and become one with Brahman, the Supreme being or Universal Self. In moksha this small self emerges into the Universal Self and becomes one.

Between Brahman, the Universal Self, and atman, the individual self, we have a kind of curtain; this veil of illusion is called maya. In Brahmanism they view Brahman (meaning God) and self as one entity; the self is eternal whether it is the individual self or the supreme self – changeless and eternal. When you become enlightened you realize salvation (moksha). In moksha this small self emerges into this big self. The curtain or veil is removed, and we (atman) become one with the Universal Self. The Buddha saw it differently. He denied the existence of this eternal, changeless self.

Buddhism tries to remind us that this empirical self, this self which is sitting here, is not real in the ultimate sense. What do we mean by no self? We are sitting here, Belinda, Ophelia, Chris, and Cindy. Aren't we each a self? Of course we are selves. Each one of us sitting here is a self, but this self changes according to the important law of the three characteristics, namely, anicca or impermanence (you cannot stay the way you are), dukkha or suffering, and finally, anatta or no self.

You look in the mirror and see yourself as beautiful. Can you tell yourself that you will stay this way forever? No. No matter how hard you try to cling to this beautiful self, it goes according to its own natural law of ageing, of decay, and death. Because of this we say that there is no such thing as an eternal self as mentioned in Brahmanism.

This is one way of understanding what we mean by no self. We take this understanding from an empirical stand. Another way of explaining non-self is by analytical means. We analyse it. Analyse what? We analyse the self, take it apart, and finally we discover that this self, the so-called self, can be separated into five 'heaps' or aggregates:

1. Form (physical body).
2. Feelings, (good, bad, and neutral).
3. Memory/perception.
4. Composition (mental composition is often the cause of suffering).
5. Consciousness (a state of knowing, which comes through six doors: eyes, ears, nose, tongue, body, and mind).

Form is what you see sitting here. You see me as Venerable Dhammananda, this is my form. By feelings I mean, good, bad, and neutral feelings, all inclusive.

Then there is this memory, perception. As soon as you see me you recognize me. 'Oh. This is Venerable Dhammananda, the nun that we met at this temple.' You see this woman, this man, you recognize him – that is perception.

Number four is composition. Composition here refers to mental composition, which is often the cause of suffering. For example, someone sees your husband walking with his secretary. This person, who bears ill will, comes and tells you, 'You know, today I saw your husband walking with his secretary.' Just the way she says it, already you feel emotional. Lots of fear, lots of mental formation, lots of imagining going on. 'Oh', you think to yourself. 'They must be going out for an evening meal. How come he is late for supper? Aah, it's because he's having supper with her', and so forth. This is mental composition, and often this type of thinking, without a basis in reality, causes so much suffering.

The fifth aggregate is consciousness. Consciousness comes through the eyes, the ears, the nose, and our senses. When you see something, consciousness and perception come together to allow you to recognize the form: perceive this is a book, this is a woman, this is a man, and so on. This is consciousness, (received) through the eyes, consciousness through the ears, through the tongue, etc. Of course, the most important of the five groupings is consciousness through the mind.

When we analyse these five aggregates for reflection, where is the self? The self is only the name. When these five elements come together, you conventionally call it the self. This is a hard concept to understand. Nagasena, a very famous monk, was asked to explain the concept of the five 'heaps' of aggregates to a Greek king, Milinda. Nagasena asked the king one question: 'You came to see me on a chariot; where is the chariot?' The king started pointing to different parts of the chariot. It's all of these parts. 'Where is the chariot?', the monk asked again.

There is no such thing as a chariot. When these different parts come together and unite in this manner, we call it a chariot. Show me your car. Some of you drove here today in a car. Exactly what is your car? Is it a wheel, a seat, is it the tyres? The car is only the name given to certain things. This is true of the self, also. When you analyse the self into the parts, you cannot see the self. Analytically, therefore, we say that there is no such thing as self. Self is a name conventionally used to call the aggregate of various components.

I offer another example, particularly for the Thai audience. It is a broom that is made from specific parts of the coconut tree. It's tied together with a string, and it's called a broom. If you remove the string that holds them together, the broom disappears. So it is with your self. As long as it is composed of these five aggregates, we supposedly call it 'this self' which works in a certain manner. But as soon as these compositions do not come together, you do not have a self. We call it the self, but in the ultimate sense the self is not there. In the analytical vein, we refuse to acknowledge the existence of self.

The concept of non-self is the most difficult concept to understand in Buddhism and to explain in such a short amount of time. It's really a challenge. It is like when we say you cannot jump into the same river twice. Suppose you take a boat tour of the Chao Phraya River, the main river in Thailand. The water which flows in the river is constantly changing because it keeps moving all the time. You may think it is the same river, but the water is different each moment. That is why we have a saying that you can never jump into the same river twice.

Yet another example is the person who came in to sit and chant and meditate. This person (I am talking about you), is it the same person who came in to chant one hour ago? Yes and no. Yes, because you are the person who walked into the room one hour ago, and no, because you have already changed within one hour. There is a medical doctor here. She can confirm that certain cells died and others were generated during the time you were here. When you came in you were not sleepy, but now you are. Changes are happening all the time.

Another way to understand the concept of no self is to understand that you cannot cling to this self as something which is eternal, which lasts for ever and ever. The idea of non-self is, in fact, a kind of mental attitude that provides you with a better understanding of nature. When you realize that nature is composed of different eco-systems that are interdependent, how can you hold on to it as something changeless, something to hang on to for ever and ever?

This kind of understanding provides a constant reminder for us not to cling unnecessarily to either pain or happiness. Everything is just a fleeting moment.

This is the real spirit of Buddhism.

CHAPTER 14

Uncertainty

That which is dependent is always uncertain.

In January of 2022, I travelled to Thailand to see Venerable Dhammananda when the COVID Omicron virus was surging and there was a lot of stress and nervousness around contagion in the airport. Everyone was on edge. A major argument broke out between a man and the flight staff while they were checking us in prior to boarding our flight. He started yelling at the attendant and I could feel everyone tensing up. The line was moving slowly, and we all worried we might not be able to board on time.

Eventually all of the passengers were seated on the plane, and we thought everything was fine until they announced that one of the pilots had tested positive for COVID. We waited for two hours on the tarmac. People were anxious and felt out of control. We were scared that the flight might be cancelled. Fortunately, they found a pilot and we were able to take off.

When I finally made it to the temple, I was relieved. Still shaken from my experience at the airport, I decided to discuss my difficulties with Venerable. I asked her, 'How do people deal with so much ongoing uncertainty in the face of the ongoing pandemic?'

She said, 'The key word I pick up just now is uncertainty. Because of uncertainty you feel you have lost control of things around you. We usually feel certain once we have the ticket in hand and board the plane that everything will be fine. The COVID situation has brought us to this new environment which says, "No, that is not true, you are not in control anymore." Even those things you think you can count on become uncertain. Like your pilot, for example. You dealt with so many obstacles at the check-in counter, and finally boarded the plane, but you could not take off because the pilot tested positive. He did not intend to get sick, it just happened. All this makes us realize things are not so certain as they seemed before COVID arrived. The pandemic really brought us into this beautiful uncertainty.'

She calmly continued, 'The Buddha already told us more than two thousand years ago that things are uncertain because they are dependent. That which is dependent is always uncertain. Even our meeting for this conversation depends on so many things of which we are unaware. Even our own breath. We are so certain that we will continue to breathe. But this breathing in and breathing out – there is a great dharma, a great teaching, a great truth here – because it is life and death right here at our nostrils.

'Breathing in, your lungs expand, and life is always inclusive; life is always smiling, life is always expanding, life is soft. But when you breathe out, when you exhale, you shrink and that is death. Life and death present themselves at every moment. We take it for granted that we will take our next breath even though people pass away quite suddenly and never get up again. It all depends on this breathing in and out. You see how immediate, how present, death is with us, but we do not realize it. We are not carefully examining the truth of life and death, both of which are right here.'

Venerable Dhammananda thought for a minute and then continued, 'In Buddhism they say anything that has this duality is not real. Inhaling and exhaling is a duality because each depends on the other. Because of this duality there is no real existence in our incoming or outgoing breath. It is a reminder of the truth that is with us all the time, yet we do not give it the importance it deserves. We do not have to look for this uncertainty – it is with us all the time with our breathing.'

I did not fully understand what she was saying about duality, so I asked her to clarify what she meant.

'Duality', she said, 'refers to things that always come together. There is black and there is white – that is duality. There is life and there is death; there is breathing in and there is breathing out. There is beauty, there is ugliness. Duality means that the thing does not exist independently because it depends on the other. Black cannot be black unless you compare it with white.'

I listened intently and then said, 'What you are really saying is that we face uncertainty in every moment.'

'True.' She nodded her head. 'Take for instance your Casual Buddhism programme – I depend on Cindy. If Cindy does not appear on my screen, we cannot do the programme no matter how prepared I am, or what I have to say. It really brings us back to the immediate present. Suppose Cindy does not show up. That is also fine with me. I do not get really upset because I understand things have this dependent nature, and the situation may change. For example, we can easily forgive a person who is two hours late once they tell us their car broke down. We understand that a person is dependent on many other factors to get here. Once we accept this, we calm down and reduce our stress. Our stress is caused by expectations; we always *expect* the perfect situation. There is no such thing as the perfect situation, and things will not always go according to our plan. When we come to this realization, we begin to cultivate an attitude of acceptance: whatever comes it is always for the best.'

Venerable Dhammananda's Teaching on Doubt

There are five obstacles or hindrances in meditation. These are sensual desire, anger and hatred, sleepiness, worry, and doubt. Doubt is when we are unsure in relation to our practice. 'The opposite of doubt is faith. When you are doubtful about whether these breathing techniques are going to help, or whether there was a Christ, or a Buddha – this kind of scepticism can be removed by faith and reasoning. When faith in Christ for the Christians and in the Buddha for Buddhists increases, our faith in our chanting and meditating reveals the goodness and kindness of the Teacher. For example, (when we meditate) we should be taking in all those (good) qualities of the Buddha within ourselves to strengthen our faith in him.'[34]

The teaching of the Buddha is so simple, much less complicated than people think. The Buddha talked about revealing the truth. In one chant we recite it says that this truth has always been there whether there was a Buddha there to discover it or not. Once in a long while, maybe once in a thousand years, a person comes along who discovers the truth. And this one person who discovered the truth is known as 'the Buddha'. But there are many Buddhas. It's as simple as that. His discovery was that the self we have been clinging to for so many lifetimes – that we cling to as if it were real – is only a shadow. What we have been doing is running after this shadow. We need to stop running for a minute and realize that this shadow is elusive. This truth is so profound and so simple that doubting your ability is also an illusion.

When we pass through all five obstacles in meditation, including doubt, and reach a stage of calm and joy, that too is an illusion. That calm joy is not yours, it's not mine, it's not me. It's such a wonderful feeling when we realize that!

CHAPTER 15

Ageing

Every time I see someone older than I am, I want to bow
as a sign of respect for the long life they have lived.

Wendy, who was a guest on Casual Buddhism, was seventy-four. She spoke about a class she was taking called 'A Year to Live', based on the book by Stephen Levine. She recited the Five Remembrances from Buddhism's Upajjhatthana Sutta – Subjects for Contemplation:[35]

> First, I am of the nature to grow old.
>> There is no way to escape growing old.
> Second, I am of the nature to have ill health.
> Third, I am of the nature to die.
> Fourth, all that is dear to me and everyone I love
>> are of the nature to change.
> Fifth, my actions are my only true belongings.

Wendy shared her thoughts with Venerable Dhammananda: 'I am looking at the time I have left to live and trying to accept growing old as a normal part of life. The class has been helpful to me in terms of dealing with my resistance. My natural tendency is to fight against the way things are because I want them to be different. But if I say *yes* to the nature of my life,

I feel more grounded and centred, which helps me feel more present – more alive. I can't fool around and waste time because this is it.'

Venerable Dhammananda nodded. 'You make a good point about feeling more alive. It is okay to grow old – ageing is a process – but at the same time you have to be in this present moment to actually feel it. We all suffer physical pain as we get older, but people often add the emotional burden of judging or blaming themselves for ageing and that is not helpful. Buddhist training helps us remove the emotional burden and anchor in the present moment.'

Wendy nodded. 'Before this conversation I attended an in-person meeting with four women I have been in a book group with and known for twenty years. One woman's husband has been diagnosed with a very severe terminal lung disease. Having known and loved this woman for so many years, I found myself feeling an exquisite, bittersweet pain that she and her husband would be going through this painful experience together.' She put her hand to her heart. 'I wanted to weep, not just because I was sad, but because I was so moved to realize that all of us will be facing a similar situation at some point.'

Venerable Dhammananda looked thoughtful and then spoke. 'Just two days ago I attended the funeral of a family friend. My mother was her grandmother's friend, so we have known each other's family for more than one hundred years. My friend was so happy to see me, she is a doctor herself, and ninety-four years old.'

Her face lit up, 'You know, even though she is a layperson, I really wanted to bow to her. Every time I see someone older than I am, I want to bow as a sign of respect for the long life they have lived. She has gone through the ageing process with such dignity. She has a very successful family – all her children are professors, and doctors. My friend sat there, *ninety-four years old*... so beautiful.'

Wendy was genuinely moved. 'That's wonderful. In our culture older people are not really honoured, respected, and appreciated. I wish they could be.'

Venerable Dhammananda lowered her gaze, 'When you know an older person well, they have stories to tell you, and we do not always listen to or value them. This older woman I spoke to recently told me about an engagement ring my mother had bought for her. My mother was the one who actually checked the diamond for her, and this woman remembered it was exactly 6.98 carats.' She shook her head in amazement. 'The details you receive from someone older than you is the kind of information you have to respect.'

Wendy nodded. 'Last year my dad died at age ninety-eight. I loved being with him and hearing his stories. Lately, I have been reviewing my life, remembering people from a long time ago. I recently reconnected with a woman I worked with during graduate school in 1974, who supervised me when I was an intern. Even though we had not seen each other for forty-eight years, when we talked, it was like no time at all had passed. We discovered we're both into horses and in recovery from substance abuse, an important part of our lives. Such an amazing connection.'

Wendy, clearly moved by the conversation, looked affectionately at Venerable Dhammananda as she continued, 'Venerable, the times I have been with you, in your presence, even across all these miles on Zoom, you touch my heart; I feel our heart connection and it makes me feel more alive and grounded. The essence of who you are is so powerful for me, such a treasure.'

Venerable Dhammananda smiled and said, 'Wendy, I attribute it all to my meditation practice. When I am sitting in front of you, I am one hundred per cent here and not distracted. That is part of samatha meditation. As I am talking to you, I am wholly here for you and that is the essence of the healing. When you are healing someone, sometimes you do not need to say anything. The person simply needs you to be present, and being connected is healing. So good to connect with you.'

Ageing in Venerable Dhammananda's Words

The Buddha talked about four noble truths, and the first truth is suffering or *dukkha*. He noticed that all human beings must go through the cycle of getting sick, getting old, and finally dying. As long as we have a physical body, we will always be experiencing some sort of suffering.

There is yet another kind of suffering which is called 'mental suffering'. Mental suffering is caused by reflection on impulses coming into the mind from the outside. It is suffering caused by our own self-delusion. Oftentimes we find that we make up stories in our heads and get so upset. No one else is doing this to us; we are doing it to ourselves.

'This is the kind of mental suffering which the Buddha professed we can overcome, namely, the suffering caused by habitual clinging to the sense of self as real. This is the wrong notion of self, which in Buddhism, we gradually learn to recognize and deny.'[36]

The process of ageing can be a painful process physically, emotionally, and mentally. We thought once we retire, we can start to enjoy life, which is true because we no longer work. But after age sixty, things start to change. Some body parts like hips and knees start to wear out. With new medical technology, many of these parts can be replaced, but some cannot.

When the physical process of decline sets in, many older people suffer from chronic pain, and that pain can cause emotional stress such as anxiety, depression, and cognitive decline. I have suffered from chronic nerve pain in my feet for more than ten years. I saw many doctors but the results were inconclusive. My problem has been difficult to diagnose but seems to originate in my brain. Apparently, my brain sends out the wrong signal to my feet. Sometimes it can be very painful, but the beautiful part is I can still function thanks to my mental training.

Having a spiritual foundation in the teachings of the Buddha helps to overcome the emotional and physical challenges of ageing. A trained mind can separate between mind and matter. The difficulty is knowing how to do that. The nature of the mind is such that it can only focus on one thing at a time. When you focus your mind on the task in front of you, the pain seems to fade into the background. For instance, if I am talking to someone, my mind is engaged in the conversation. The pain is still there, but the mind is not taking in that information, so the pain diminishes. With awareness I can clearly see that the pain is in my feet, not in my mind. Coping with the challenges of ageing becomes much easier when we practise the dharma.

PART III

The Light of Our Beings – Reflections on the Ordained Life

This last section deals with monastic experience. I call it 'the light of our beings' because receiving temporary ordination is like being initiated into a different world, one in which I experience the sacred abundance of life. In the chapter that follows I write about my most recent ordination to demystify the experience for people who are curious to know more about what it was like. The book concludes with Venerable Dhammananda's invaluable thoughts and reflections on the past two decades of her ordained life.

CHAPTER 16

Wearing the Robe

When you wear the robes, you bear the responsibility of people's faith, you carry their burdens, hopes, and dreams in your hands.

Every December since 2016 I have made an annual pilgrimage to Thailand to visit Venerable Dhammananda. Coming to the temple is like coming home to myself; it is where the missing puzzle pieces of who I am fall into place and the picture that is me makes sense.

It may sound strange to travel ten thousand miles to a country where I do not speak the language to find myself, but that is how it has always been. When I sit in the presence of my spiritual teacher I become whole. I guess you could say my heart expands in response to her love; I become a more authentic, happier, joyful version of myself.

I am fortunate to have this close relationship with Venerable Dhammananda, who in December 2022 celebrated twenty years of ordination and became a *mahatheri* – most venerated senior nun. In anticipation of this special occasion, I decided to honour her by taking temporary ordination as a samaneri.

I had taken temporary ordination once before in 2014, so I thought I had a pretty good idea of what to expect. Being ordained the first time was fun. I was the only English-speaking person among 122 Thai women who doted over me as the only *farang* or foreigner. I loved the experience, but because all the instructions were given in Thai, I did not understand the significance of what I was doing. I felt like a child, dependent on my sisters to guide me. People cried out, '*Khun* Cindy, over here!' They took my arm and led me back when I wandered from my assigned space in line. When it came time to recite the most important chant asking Venerable Dhammananda for ordination I sat quietly with my eyes closed and palms pressed together. I was play-acting the part, not fully present. After my ordination I returned home elated. Friends commented that I radiated an inner glow they had never seen before. I assumed this would happen again, but, as it turned out, my first experience did little to prepare me for the second one.

The month prior to leaving, I spoke to Venerable Dhammananda over Zoom about how excited I was to receive ordination again. She became serious. 'This is your second time, so I expect you to recite the chants along with the others.' My heart sank. *How would I memorize twenty minutes of Pali chanting ahead of time?* Fortunately, someone from the temple sent me a recording of a woman reciting the verses. I practised diligently and after three weeks had practically memorized the entire recitation. Even so, I felt pressured. What if I froze during the ceremony and botched it? The stage was being set, and my initial excitement about being ordained shifted to apprehension.

I was not only worried about the chanting. Because of my age, seventy-one, I knew that living for three weeks at the temple would be a physical challenge. As Venerable

Dhammananda often said, 'Living in a monastery is not for everyone.' Temple life is dirty feet caked with a layer of dust from walking in flip flops on patches of earth and concrete walkways. It is hot and humid days, followed by warm sleepless nights lying on a two-inch foam mattress covered in grey plastic with an overhead fan swirling above the bed, and waking at 4.30 a.m. for early morning chanting.

I sensed the drama building in my mind and tried to counter the negativity by focusing on the possibilities. This was, after all, an opportunity to honour my teacher while deepening my commitment to Buddhism. I knew instinctively that no matter what challenges arose, I would meet them. My attitude began to improve. By the time I left for Bangkok I was hopeful that the experience would be positive.

I arrived on the last day of November. I caught a taxi and the closer we got to the temple the more excited I became. I craned my neck, searching for the familiar Chinese Buddha seated at the front entrance.

'*Leyo sigh*! Turn left!' I exclaimed, and the driver made a sharp left turn through the temple gates. I went straight to the main office to pick up my room key. Luang Pi Kiccha, the bhikkhuni at the front desk, handed me a key and told me Venerable Dhammananda was expecting me. I rolled my suitcase down the concrete pathway and found her seated with her elder sister in her favourite meeting place, the shaded area underneath the dormitory.

Venerable Dhammananda pictured with her elder sister in December 2022

I was happy to see Venerable Dhammananda and greeted her with the traditional Thai *wai*, bowing at the waist three times and pressing my palms together at my forehead to signal my deep respect. She smiled and said, 'You must be tired. Go rest and we'll talk later.'

On the way to my room, I met Daphne, one of two American women living at the temple, conducting fieldwork for her PhD studies. I had never visited when English-speaking guests were there, so this was a treat. The other eighteen candidates seeking ordination were Thai and would be arriving soon. I was the eldest participant and the only non-Thai speaker.

When all the candidates arrived, we began preparing for ordination. We were given our *civara*s or robes. I revered the garment but was also intimidated by it. At first glance the robe is a patchwork of larger and smaller squares and rectangles sewn together into one long piece of fabric. The trick is there's a top and bottom to the garment, but for the life of me I could not distinguish between them to identify the starting point from which to fold it properly. When worn correctly, a *civara* is wrapped snugly around the body and neatly draped over the left shoulder in clean, even folds, but I struggled every time and needed help putting it on.

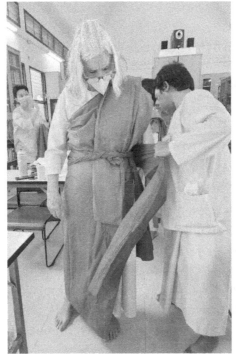

Practising folding and wearing the robe for temporary ordination in December 2022

Over the next two days during practice sessions, my apprehension began to build. Not having a roommate, I wondered how I would manage to fold my robe in the morning without a partner. I did not like having to depend on others. The worry did not stop there. I was filled with dread about two future events involving the robe. Although we started out dressed in white, midway through the ceremony we would approach Venerable Dhammananda individually, bow before her on our knees and offer her our orange robes, which we balanced on our opened palms. She would then untie a strap wrapped around the robe and drape it around our neck. The ritual is significant because, symbolically, it represents Venerable Dhammananda passing the lineage down to us and granting us permission to wear the robe. I dreaded this exchange because I have bad knees. I was pretty sure I could kneel while balancing the robes but was not sure my legs were strong enough to stand up without the use of my arms. I imagined the worst-case scenario, stuck on the ground with everyone watching, I would be mortified.

After that exchange, we would exit and go downstairs to remove our white clothing and change into our orange robes. My greatest fear was that I would not be able to change in time. I imagined being tangled in a mass of cloth, while everyone else managed fine. Even though people had reassured me on numerous occasions that there would be plenty of volunteers to help us, I was not convinced. I envisioned myself struggling with my robe while everyone else lined up neatly dressed to walk back to the vihara, leaving me behind. I was clearly having a hard time.

We held a final rehearsal the day before our ordination. We chanted the Pali verses asking for *pabbajjam* lower ordination, which in Pali literally means 'going forth':

Aham aye pabbajjam yacami
[Venerable (feminine form), I request the going-forth]
Dutiyampi aham aye pabbajjam yacami
[For a second time, I request the going-forth]
Tatiyampi aham aye pabbajjam yacami
[For a third time, I request the going-forth]

*Sabba dukkha nissarana nibbana sacchikaranatthaya imam
kasayam gahetva pabbajeth mam aye anukampam upadaya*
[For the sake of escape from all suffering and for the
realization of nirvana, taking this robe, Venerable, out of
compassion, please grant me the going-forth]

*Dutiyampi Sabba dukkha nissarana nibbana
sacchikaranatthaya imam kasayam gahetva pabbajeth
mam aye anukampam upadaya* [For a second time, for the
sake of escape from all suffering and for the realization of
nirvana, taking this robe, Venerable, out of compassion,
please grant me the going-forth]

*Tatiyampi Sabba dukkha nissarana nibbana
sacchikaranatthaya imam kasayam gahetva pabbajeth mam
aye anukampam upadaya* [For a third time, for the sake of
escape from all suffering and for the realization of nirvana,
taking this robe, Venerable, out of compassion, please grant
me the going-forth] (Translation by Dhivan Thomas Jones)

When the moment came to approach Venerable Dhammananda
and offer her my robe, I slowly lowered myself down. She
draped the tie around my neck, but I struggled to get up. She
seemed surprised and said, 'Oh. That is hard for you.' She
extended her hand to help me. I felt embarrassed but also
grateful that she was so understanding. I was not sure how
we would handle this part during the actual ceremony, but I
instinctively trusted Dhammananda would guide me.

As the rehearsal progressed, Venerable Dhammananda grew
irritated because the straps were not wrapped properly around
all of our robes, and she could not untie them easily. Exasperated,

she tugged at the ties one by one until everyone had finished. Afterwards she turned to us with a serious expression and gave us instruction. As newly ordained *samaneri*s, we represented the bhikkhuni sangha, 'As a monastic you depend on your livelihood from laypeople. Therefore, you have to be very proper in your behaviour and the way you present yourself to the public. When you wear the robes, you bear the responsibility of people's faith, you carry their burdens, hopes and dreams in your hands.' Most important, she added, 'Be humble.'

The next day, 5 December 2022, was our ordination. I woke at 4.30 a.m. to prepare for early morning chanting at 5.30. Everyone was dressed in a white shirt and skirt, and a cape called a *sabai*. The white signified that we were laywomen who had taken on eight precepts.

I am with Richie, my Thai translator, whose English was perfect – I would have been lost without her

At 7 a.m., the group gathered inside the library, while outside, near the temple entrance, parents (or close relatives) arrived to support their daughters through the ordination process. Thai people believe it is important for children to honour their parents by taking ordination, and it is a very emotional time for everyone involved. Inside the library, we preened over one another, adjusting our capes, and making sure we looked our best. A volunteer stood in front of the group and talked about forgiveness. She said that whatever hurt we may have caused another person intentionally or unintentionally in the past, to think about that person, ask for their forgiveness, and then let it go.

Venerable Dhammananda later explained that this was a time of spiritual purification before we shaved our heads. 'There is a lot of crying', she said, 'daughters ask their parents for forgiveness, and when they do, a physical release happens freeing them from all the guilt and tension they have held onto for so many years.'

At 7.30 a.m. we took our places in line. We were arranged by height. At 5 feet 7 inches I was the tallest person, so I was at the end of the line. Knowing we were about to start, my anxiety really took off. Even with rehearsals, I was unsure of myself because I did not speak Thai. I was afraid I would step out of line or bow at the wrong time or make some obvious mistake. My nerves were jangled. Not only that, but Thai people can be extremely curious about foreigners, and I knew they would be watching me closely.

We walked to the concrete walkway in front of the main temple, a wide-open concrete space. An aisle had been cleared and we made our way to three rows of seats on our left. The parents sat across the aisle from us. At the far end of the aisle an ornate chair had been placed under an awning for Venerable Dhammananda. After everyone was settled, she walked in, and we all stood to offer the traditional Thai greeting, *wai*.

We recited a chant asking the parents for forgiveness and they responded with a different chant asking their daughters for forgiveness. Thai volunteers circulated among the candidates handing out lotus blossoms. Next, everyone got up from their seats and went to kneel before their parents and present the flowers. Since I had no family members present, I had been told beforehand to bow before Venerable Dhammananda. Once again, I was concerned about my knees.

I approached Venerable Dhammananda and prepared to kneel. As I did, she stood up. I was shocked. It is almost unheard of for a bhikkhuni to stand to receive a layperson, especially in public. Thai people revere monastics and bow low on their knees in their presence. Venerable Dhammananda made a huge exception. I was overcome with humility and moved by her kindness.

With my head lowered she whispered, 'You are a very kind-hearted person, so I doubt you have hurt someone deeply, but if you have, think about that person now and ask for their forgiveness.' My eyes got teary as I thought about my former husband of thirty-three years, and how deeply I had hurt him when I asked for a divorce. I mentally asked him to forgive me and silently began to cry as I returned to my seat.

The next thing I knew, a volunteer handed me a large lotus leaf to cover my lap. Everyone waited as Venerable approached to cut the first lock of hair. When she came to me, she said, 'This is to remove the mental defilements.'

Bowing before Venerable Dhammananda prior to having my head shaved during the ordination ceremony, December 2022

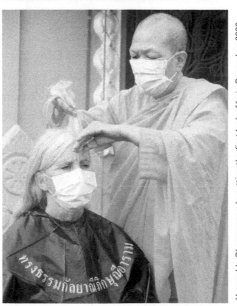

Venerable Dhammananda cutting the first lock of hair, December 2022

Soon after, parents, relatives, and members of the temple came with scissors to cut more hair. I waited patiently as people approached me with kind looks in their eyes and asked for permission to cut my hair. Thais believe clipping the hair is auspicious and they gain merit (or good karma) from doing it. When enough of my hair was cut, I went to a designated area where women waited with electric shavers to remove the rest of my hair.

Everything proceeded smoothly after that, and my confidence began to build. We formed a single line and walked in slow procession to the back garden to the Medicine Buddha vihara. Venerable Dhammananda was seated in front of the room and the women took their places facing her on mats. I was allowed to sit in a low chair. When my turn came to offer Venerable Dhammananda my robe, she told me to simply bend forward while standing in front of her. My worry melted into relief.

As for the quick clothing change out of my white clothing into the robe, I was helped by a woman who efficiently tucked and pulled the robe in all the right places, so it fitted perfectly. For the first time, I began to enjoy the ordination process and realized everything had turned out fine – I recited the verses properly, my robe looked fantastic, and within a few minutes the ceremony would be over, or so I thought.

We exited the vihara and stepped outside to receive our alms bowl. Each woman had been paired with a volunteer ahead of time, so we lined up face-to-face with our assigned person. The man standing in front of me held a black lacquer bowl. Since a female nun cannot have direct contact with a man, I leaned forward and extended the lower sash of my robe, and he placed the bowl on top of it. I wrapped my fingers snugly around the bowl making sure not to drop it. Then we turned in unison and walked in procession from the back garden to the main entrance of the temple.

As we approached the front, I assumed we were almost finished, but the woman ahead of me suddenly stopped. I looked up and and saw an endless receiving line of Thais waiting to offer us food and donations. We inched forward and with each step I grew more anxious. Soon I came face to face with a Thai man who smiled, looked directly into my eyes and with deep appreciation, bowed. That is when I panicked! *This man reveres me*. My stomach churned and pangs of doubt surfaced. *Who am I to deserve his respect?* I felt like an impostor. Here I was emulating being a peaceful, calm, Buddhist while feeling like a hot mess inside. I recalled a phrase a friend had taught me: *I am worthy... I am worthy.* This became my mantra as I progressed through the line.

One by one, I accepted people's offerings. I reminded myself to breathe as I moved in close to an elderly woman who handed me a stem of orchids. Next, a little boy who was no more than five years old looked up at me with adoring eyes. He held a package of sweets but struggled to reach the inside of my alms bowl. I bent down and waited patiently as he stuffed the treat inside. I do not recall specific faces or details after that as I waded through the crowd, but I do remember people's smiles and the warmth in their eyes as they made their offerings. When I reached the final person, I heaved a huge sigh of relief and relaxed.

The highlight of my ordination experience happened a few days later when the entire group went on a dawn alms round, called *bindabat* in Thai. This practice dates back to the

Buddha's time and benefits both the ordained monks and the laity. Monks depend on the local people for food, and in return the locals receive spiritual guidance from them.

People in the community wake early to cook rice and other foods for the ordained women. By offering food, they are practising generosity and with these acts of kindness they are generating good karma. Many Thais believe in karma and rebirth and that the actions they perform in their current life will have an effect on their next life. By giving alms, the locals are building good karma for their future.

The monastic women at Wat Songdhammakalyani go on alms round between 6 and 7 a.m. every Sunday and on Buddhist holy days. The day our group went out for alms was a Sunday. We lined up according to height and exited the temple gates in partial darkness. As we turned off the main highway to a side street, word spread fast among the local community that a procession of twenty-seven women, novices and fully ordained bhikkhunis, carrying alms bowls, was approaching. Excited onlookers ran to catch a glimpse of us and then darted back inside to grab rice, water, packages of food – whatever they could get their hands on – to offer alms. It was kind of like a flash mob, a wave of people that swelled and gained momentum as we made our way down the street. People were overjoyed to see us, and we received almost four times more food than we normally collected. The cart carrying donations was overflowing.

The people's acceptance was heart-warming and indicated how much more public support there is today for ordained women than there was twenty years ago when Venerable Dhammananda, a newly ordained novice, was criticized in the press. I was filled with hope that her dream to revive the bhikkhuni sangha in her homeland would become a reality.

Alms round December 2022

*

Despite the trepidation I experienced during my second ordination, I was proud of myself for having completed the ceremony and felt good afterwards. I would sum up my experience in one word: *initiation*. For me the word 'initiation' meant a new beginning and marked my transformation into a new way of life. When I came home it was as if a veil had been lifted from my eyes, and reality came into focus. I began to see which relationships were fulfilling me and which were not. I made choices about how and with whom I wanted to spend time.

Although the ordination process was intense, afterwards I experienced a deeper sense of connection to myself. My lens of understanding shifted to embrace a broader acceptance of who I am, what I wanted and needed. I no longer felt a need to apologize for my decisions, I simply pursued what I wanted with a clear conscience.

I thought back to my experience in the receiving line and was surprised I had panicked. Perhaps I felt the full impact of what Venerable Dhammananda meant when she said, 'Be humble.' I felt people's love and respect as I accepted their offerings and sensed the weight of my responsibility to carry their faith forward. I was filled with humility by their kindness. Ultimately, I came to appreciate the seriousness with which Venerable Dhammananda regarded ordination and understood the importance of the bhikkhuni sangha earning people's respect.

If I were to ordain again, I would probably try to worry less and be more present. One of the biggest lessons for me was the experience of wearing the robe. I had an unrealistic expectation that I had to do it all myself. I wasted so much time and stress, when, in reality, someone was always ready and willing to help. Venerable Dhammananda said, 'If we cannot learn to rely on others, we will suffer.' This was my takeaway. Especially at my age, I want to accept it is okay to ask for help when I need it.

In hindsight, when I reflect on my two ordination experiences I realize they were quite different. The first time I wore the robes, I felt very comfortable in them. I even considered becoming a bhikkhuni; however, I chose to return to my lay life. One important distinction Venerable Dhammananda likes to make is that a person does not have to be ordained to achieve enlightenment. I have often heard her say, 'Being a monastic does not guarantee enlightenment. Lay people can also be enlightened.' For me, being a dedicated practitioner is enough of a commitment.

I consider myself lucky to have a permanent home with my teacher at Wat Songdhammakalyani, a place where I am always welcome. I treasure my annual visits to Thailand and carry the spirit of love I receive from Venerable Dhammananda, the Thai people, and the other ordained women at the Temple back home with me.

Newly ordained, December 2022

CHAPTER 17

Reflections on the Ordained Life

There are very few monks who support us.

A week after our temporary novice ordination, our group attended a celebration at the Bangkok Arts and Culture Centre to honour Venerable Dhammananda for being the first fully ordained Theravada bhikkhuni in Thailand, and for her twenty years of ordination. She received a new honorific title and became a *mahatheri*, which means 'most venerated one', or 'great one'.

I was seated in the audience with the other twenty samaneris in the third row of the auditorium for this auspicious occasion. As the famous Thai monk Phra Alongkot Tikkapanyo, who is known for his dedicated service providing care for HIV/AIDS patients, joined Venerable Dhammananda on stage, she quietly turned towards the audience, teared up, and in a near whisper said, 'There are very few monks who support us.' Hearing her say this had a profound effect on me. I realized how much courage it must have taken for Venerable Dhammananda to be the first woman to walk the path, and how difficult her journey must have been.

Venerable Dhammananda in 2022

A few days after the celebration in Bangkok, I spoke with Venerable Dhammananda about her reflections on twenty years of ordination. We met in the temple library, a light-filled space. There is a huge golden statue of the Buddha's devoted disciple Ananda in front of the room. We always bow to Ananda when we first enter. The library is the space where the nuns come to receive instruction. They sit at six-foot-long metal tables in black plastic chairs. The back area is full of bookshelves lined with stacks of books that date back to Venerable Dhammananda's mother's time.

Our meeting took place mid-afternoon. The sunlight streamed in through floor-length windows and the room was hot. I went around and turned on all the fans to cool it down. When Venerable Dhammananda arrived she was quiet, not her usual talkative self. She looked tired. The past two weeks had been very busy, starting with the ordination of the samaneris and ending with the celebration in Bangkok.

She took a seat at the table. 'Let us begin', was all she said. I had heard it had been particularly difficult securing a keynote speaker for the recent event and asked Venerable Dhammananda about this.

'You know, even though the initial controversy surrounding my ordination has calmed down, the "bhikkhuni issue" is still a contentious one in Thailand. Ten months ago, my assistant, Khun Kanjana, invited the Sri Lankan Ambassador to Thailand to be the keynote speaker, but she backed out just ten days before the event. She was probably scared of the political backlash from supporting the bhikkhuni and did not want to antagonize anyone.

'We really had to scurry to get another speaker and approached the Sri Lankan monk Most Venerable B. Sri Sarankara Nayaka Maha Thera. He is the Chief High Priest of the Adhikarana Sangha Nayaka of Malaysia, and founder of the Maha Karuna Buddhist Society. He graciously agreed to be the keynote speaker and arrived at very short notice. It was not easy to secure his visa, we had to scramble, but we had some personal connections at the embassy who helped us out.'

I remember being impressed by the Sri Lankan monk. He was a tall man with a regal presence. When he took the stage, he spoke in a quiet, dignified manner. He was so confident in his delivery, no one would ever have suspected that he only had three days to prepare.

I asked Venerable Dhammananda to comment on her reflections as a bhikkhuni for the past two decades. 'Looking back on your experience, what have you learned and what thoughts would you like to share today?'

She picked up her phone and scrolled through some photos. 'I think this photo is important because it shows my interest in ordination started early. I learned all the chanting I teach the samaneris now when I was twelve years old. Just like my mother, I received the eight precepts and wore the light-yellow robe. At that time, I was on summer vacation for forty-seven days. I was nervous about going back to school with my head shaved, but all the other students treated me with kindness. They never teased me, so I was really blessed to have a good group of friends in my school days. The idea of ordination was planted in me a long time ago.'

Young Chatsumarn Kabilsingh, age twelve, pictured in the right foreground

'Now back to the other part of your question, what have I learned? The establishment of the bhikkhuni sangha must be done properly, must be done in public, and must be done with sufficient training. The last point is key, ordination must be combined with training.

'After receiving higher ordination, a bhikkhuni must receive training from her teacher for two years or *vassa*s [rain retreats].

In 2003 it was difficult for me to travel to Sri Lanka to be with my teacher Venerable Saddha Sumana, because my mother was ninety-three, and I could not possibly leave her. So, I invited my teacher to stay with us at our temple.

'Venerable Saddha Sumana accepted my invitation because in her *arama* [living space] there were only two ordained women, herself and a samaneri, so there was no *patimokkha* recitation [ritual chanting of the 311 monastic rules for women] because to do this you need to have at least four bhikkhunis. It's important to recite the Patimokkha so that we can adhere to the monastic rules in our practice.

'When Venerable Santini from Indonesia and Venerable Dhammanandi from Viet Nam heard that we were offering training during the vassa, they asked if they could join us. We agreed they could come, and two more ordained women from Sri Lanka joined us as well. There were six of us altogether, which made it possible for us to recite the Patimokkha. I was very happy about this.'[37]

'My mother's death on June 24, 2003, coincided with the arrival of the foreign bhikkhuni for our rains retreat. We kept her body on the ground floor of the monastery for about one hundred days before her cremation.'[38] 'For the next three months, we all gathered around her body in the evening to recite the funeral chants for the dead in Pali.

'We cremated her on 5 October 2003. We hired a royal carriage to transport her body and the bhikkhunis sat on the four corners surrounding her. It was dark all day. The sky was closed. Then we circled the crematorium three times, and when we were done, we lifted her coffin up to the crematorium platform. As soon as we did, the sky opened. It was miraculous, so beautiful.

'After we cremated her, we had another ceremony. The provincial chief monk came to hand certificates to the international bhikkhunis for having completed the training for the funeral recitation. The bhikkhunis learned how to perform a proper funeral service for a senior nun. Once again, my emphasis was on training. The women stayed through until the *kathina*. Kathina marks the end of vassa with the official robes offering ceremony.'

Venerable Dhammananda's tone shifted. She became quiet and said, 'I'll make a confession to you. The purpose of all our struggles from my mother's time to my time was to start a sangha. The first two years I was ordained [2001–3] I really had trouble with my sangha because I was only thinking of myself as the centre of the universe. There was a lot of misunderstanding. The sangha was having difficulties.

'In terms of my own spiritual growth, I did not know I was very judgemental, and this is my confession. I was self-centred and criticized people according to my standards. If someone was not doing something the way I wanted, I viewed them harshly. It was a revelation for me. I did not realize I was a privileged person, that I had a privileged upbringing with my family and a good education in a private school.

'I was the only child in my family, and apart from my mother, I never had to listen to anyone. Then I became a professor, and everyone had to listen to *me*. So, I could not help being like that. I recognized I was the problem because I did not respect others. I always judged them from a position of power because I was senior and thought I knew better – was better educated, et cetera.

'But when I started to practise the dharma, I wanted to start a sangha and knew I could not be like that. I began to ask myself, "How do I nourish my sangha?" That is when I realized I needed to change, and once I did the situation began to improve. It is vital we recognize the importance of creating sangha and to do that we must respect others as much as ourselves. I always have to set the standard for the sangha, but I need to be patient and allow them to grow. I need compassion to appreciate the other person's perspective. This is dharma practice. It is not easy, but there is that recognition that we respect the sangha and slowly it is coming along.'

There was a pause in the conversation. Venerable Dhammananda was silent and closed her eyes for a moment. It was warm in the library, and she had been talking for quite a while. I waited a few minutes and then continued our conversation. I had heard her say that this is the beginning of the third decade of Theravada bhikkhunis in Thailand, and the start of a new chapter. I asked if she had any specific hopes or dreams for the future.

'I would like to see the bhikkhunis come out of their shell and reach out to the public. We need to be seen doing good things so that we gain public recognition. As the Buddha said to the very first batch of sixty enlightened monks whom he sent out to preach, "Be beneficial to yourselves, and be beneficial to others."

'I spoke about my early experiences with my sangha and how I looked inward to evaluate my own actions. If we can't do self-evaluation, we become the problem. Be sincere in your self-evaluation so that you can reach out to other bhikkhunis. By reaching out, you are helping to support the bhikkhuni sangha and then they can start supporting the larger public. This goes hand in hand.

'In the third decade I hope to see that the bhikkhunis are much more committed to right livelihood. We shave our heads, we wear the robes, we are the bhikkhunis. What do we do as bhikkhunis? Are we sincere in our right livelihood? Are we sincere in our commitment to let go of clinging and attachment? Are we sincere in our path, seeking refuge in the Buddha. Are we living simply and sharing what we have with others? For example, we receive a lot of donations as monastics including feminine hygiene products. All the bhikkhunis living here are older and do not need these products any longer. We have a programme where the bhikkhunis go into local prisons and teach meditation to the female prisoners. We donate the excess of feminine hygiene products to the prison.'

At this point I shifted the focus of conversation back to the celebration in Bangkok. 'I want to ask you about a poignant moment in the ceremony, when you sat with Phra Alongkot Tikkapanyo and spoke about how very few Thai monks have supported you. Have the Thai monks' attitudes changed in the past twenty years?'

'You know, we have been meeting with male professors at the local university twice a month and they tell me that the younger generation of monks has no problem with the bhikkhuni at all. It is only the senior officials in the sangha who have problems.

'In the past twenty years I never behaved in any way that presented a threat to the bhikkhus. I always expressed my respect for the bhikkhus. I correct the Thai people when they say the bhikkhus have only 227 precepts and the bhikkhunis have 311 precepts, therefore the bhikkhunis are considered higher. I tell them, "no". The bhikkhunis are younger sisters to the bhikkhus.

'This is according to the history. The bhikkhunis came into existence five years after the bhikkhus. In that sense we are always junior to the bhikkhus. Phra Alongkot is only in his sixties, and I am sixteen years his senior, but I always pay respect to him. I have no problem paying respect to the bhikkhus.

'There are exceptions to this, however: if a particular bhikkhu has shown improper behaviour or been disrespectful to a bhikkhuni, we do not have to pay our respects. For the bhikkhunis if we are not respectful, the bhikkhus will not give instruction. Within this brother and sister relationship, there is an invisible line of understanding separating the bhikkhus and the bhikkhunis as well as uniting us. We are the same sangha. When we have both bhikkhus and bhikkhunis in the audience I address them as "maha sanghas", which means both bhikkhuni and bhikkhu sangha.

'Back to your question about the monks' attitude towards us; they are much more open and accepting. But the year I was ordained, I saw how nasty people could be. There was one radio talk show host in particular who chose the harshest criticism and played it over and over again. So, people who had not listened to the programme regularly thought there were many people who were against the bhikkhuni. I challenged them and told them this is my address, please come and visit my temple and see for yourself. No one came. I believe that whatever the unwholesome mind generates will destroy itself. I really believe that. If you do things out of *kusula citta* [wholesome mind], the wholesomeness will nourish you.

'People can say all sorts of nasty things, but I am not responsible for them. I know myself and what I do. I keep on doing wholesome things and keep to the path – as monastics we continue to do what is expected of us. After twenty years, people have seen that the bhikkhunis are not here to harm society or destroy Buddhism. So far, we are steadfast in our wholesome mind expressed through our wholesome actions. I think this is the energy which will put us on the right track.'

I had one last question. 'What final thoughts would you like to leave us with today?'

Venerable Dhammananda rocked gently from left to right as if gathering momentum. 'The Bhikkhuni sangha is relatively new in Thailand and neighbouring countries Vietnam and Indonesia. It just came about in the past three decades. Therefore, we are starting a new page of history. May this young tree, this young sapling of bhikkhunis be strong and prosper so that we can strengthen Buddhism in the future.'

Crack in the Wall of Patriarchy

I am but a small crack in the wall,
The wall of patriarchy,
The wall of hierarchy,
The wall of injustice.

Suddenly there are many more cracks!
Eventually the wall crumpled.

Lo, and behold,
the Buddha is standing on the other side,
With his opened arms
to welcome his daughters,
Who struggled to keep up the heritage,
The heritage given by the Buddha.

Bhikkhuni Dhammananda, 2005

Afterword

I spoke about the 'crack in the wall of patriarchy' in a speech I gave at Thammasat University in 2005. The phrase 'crack in the wall of patriarchy' originated with the Nobel Peace Prize Committee. At that time, the committee was seeking nominations for 1,000 'peace women' who, collectively, would receive the Nobel Prize. Of the 2,000 candidates nominated I was selected. The idea was that if many small cracks joined together, eventually the wall would topple.

The speech I wrote was based on a story about a Buddha statue in Bodh Gaya in the tenth century. At that time India was occupied by Muslims. One day a Muslim captain rode by on horseback, looked through a temple doorway, and saw a statue of the Buddha inside. Since the Muslim religion does not believe in idolatry, the officer asked the abbot to remove the Buddha statue. That night the abbot called his attendants to a meeting. He asked them to do something in secret. The three attendants built a wall in front of the Buddha statue to hide it. When the Muslim captain returned two days later, he saw the statue was gone.

No one at the temple spoke about what they had done. About one hundred years later, some women were cleaning and they discovered a small crack in the wall. Through the crack they could see something shiny, so they started to remove the barrier and discovered the beautiful Buddha statue hidden inside.

As Buddhists, we must remove this wall of patriarchy, hierarchy, and injustice. This is how I teach students in my class about deconstruction, how we need to deconstruct that which becomes an obstacle to our practice, to our understanding of the Buddha's teachings, and to follow the Vinaya properly.

In the twenty years I have been ordained, I have grown to appreciate that change cannot happen overnight. It took years for the destructive social attitudes barring women from certain activities to form, and it will take time to deconstruct them. If you study religion, you will discover that, previously, there was a matriarchal society in which the Mother Goddess was revered for her role in taking care of the earth and the environment. Our society may have been in the hands of men for too long. It is our responsibility to clean up the spiritual mess left behind.

A society in which women have been suppressed for so long is not easily changed. As Buddhists it is our responsibility to fight against injustice. We must remove this wall of illusion, this wall of patriarchy, hierarchy, and inequity to see the truth of the Buddha's teachings. Whether the oppression is political, social, religious – whatever – we have to think hard about it together, not separately. The extent to which we can think collectively and commit together is the extent to which we can bring about social change.

Bhikkhuni Dhammananda

Notes

Introduction: A Healing Presence

1 Cindy Rasicot, *Finding Venerable Mother: A Daughter's Spiritual Quest to Thailand*, She Writes Press, Berkeley 2020, pp.9–10.

2 Bhikkhu Analayo, 'The legality of Bhikkhuni ordination', *Journal of Buddhist Ethics* 20 (2013), p.311.

3 Dr Chatsumarn Kabilsingh, *Thai Women in Buddhism*, Parallax Press, Berkeley 1991, p.36.

4 Bhikkhu Analayo, *Bhikkhuni Ordination from Ancient India to Contemporary Sri Lanka,* Agama Research Group, Taiwan 2023, p.14.

5 Koun Franz, *The Fourfold Assembly*, 2021, available at https://dharmacrafts.com/blogs/news/the-fourfold-assembly-koun-franz, accessed on 10 June 2023.

6 Bhikkhu Analayo, *Bhikkhuni Ordination from Ancient India to Contemporary Sri Lanka*, p.30.

7 Rasicot, *Finding Venerable Mother*, p.86.

1   The Rebel Monk

8 Bhikkhuni Dhammananda, *The Bhikkhuni Lineage*, first published as a paper pamphlet, Nakhon Pathom 2004, p.12.

9 *Sri Krung*, 'Aiyakan forng nen phu-laew' (Prosecutor Files a Case Against Female Novices), 6 September 1929, from National Archives R7 M26.5/248. This citation is taken from Varaporn Chamsanit, 'Reconnecting the Lost Lineage: Challenges to Institutional Denial of Buddhist Women's Monasticism in Thailand', PhD thesis, Australian National University, October 2006, p.77.

10 Chamsanit, 'Reconnecting the Lost Lineage', p.78. See note 9.

11 Bhikkhuni Dhammananda, *The Bhikkhuni Lineage*, p.19.

12 Kabilsingh, *Thai Women in Buddhism*, p.52.

13 Bhikkhuni Dhammananda, *The Bhikkhuni Lineage*, p.13.

14 Kabilsingh, *Thai Women in Buddhism*, p.52.

15 Atiya Achakulwisut, 'Her holiness', *Bangkok Post*, 30 May 2001, available at https://www.budsas.org/ebud/ebdha220a.htm, accessed on 20 March 2023.

16 Ibid.

17 Bhikkhu Analayo, 'The legality of bhikkhuni ordination', pp.313–14.

18 Sanitsuda Ekachai, 'The Dhammananda controversy', *Bangkok Post*, 22 September 2001, available at https://www.budsas.org/ebud/ebdha220a.htm, accessed on 20 March 2023.

19 Chamsanit, 'Reconnecting the Lost Lineage', p.205.

20 Achakulwisut, 'Her holiness'.

21 Atiya Achakulwisut, 'A path less travelled', *Bangkok Post*, 17 April 2001, available at https://www.budsas.org/ebud/ebdha220a.htm, accessed on 20 March 2023.

22 Bhikkhuni Dhammananda, 'Three waves of Bhikkhuni sangha in Thailand', *Yasodhara* 19:4 (July–September 2003), pp.5–7. (*Yasodhara* was the title of the temple newsletter, which was published quarterly for thirty years from 1984 to 2014.)

23 Chamsanit, 'Reconnecting the Lost Lineage', pp.165–6.

24 Statement of His Holiness the Dalai Lama on Bhikshuni Ordination in the Tibetan Tradition, 20 July 2007, available at https://web.archive.org/web/20170326094227/http://www.congress-on-buddhist-women.org/index.php?id=142, accessed on 1 March 2023.

25 Ibid.

2 Healing the Mother–Daughter Relationship

26 Rasicot, *Finding Venerable Mother*, p.182.

27 Ibid., p.95.

3 The Turning Point

28 Rasicot, *Finding Venerable Mother*, p.90.

29 By 1983 Chatsumarn Kabilsingh was being recognized

internationally as an expert in women's ordination issues. Many Buddhist nuns and women from around the world began to correspond with her. When she received more requests than she could handle, she decided to issue a quarterly publication called *Newsletter on International Buddhist Women's Activities* (NIBWA). Only thirty copies were mailed in the first edition; however, within five years circulation had increased to reach recipients in twenty-seven countries. The newsletter was later renamed *Yasodhara* (wife of the Buddha) and was published until 2014 when Dhammananda realized there was less of a need for it with the advent of social media.

Chatsumarn Kabilsingh's networking efforts paid off. In 1987, working in collaboration with Venerable Ayya Khema and Karma Lekshe Tsomo, she co-founded Sakyadhita (daughters of the Buddha), an international association of Buddhist women. The first conference was held in Bodh Gaya and featured His Holiness the Dalai Lama as the keynote speaker. The conference brought together Buddhist laywomen, nuns, and monks from different countries to discuss relevant topics related to Buddhist women. Since 1987, Sakyadhita has convened conferences in thirteen countries and increased its membership to approximately 2,000. Dhammananda was elected President of Sakyadhita in 1991 and served until 1993.

6 Meditation

30 Rasicot, *Finding Venerable Mother*, p.91.
31 Bhikkhuni Dhammananda, *Training the Monkey Mind*, Kledthai, Bangkok 2008, p.39.
32 Bhikkhuni Dhammananda, *Training the Monkey Mind*, p.8.

8 Forgiveness

33 Bhikkhuni Dhammananda, *Training the Monkey Mind*, pp.42–3.

14 Uncertainty

34 Bhikkhuni Dhammananda, *Training the Monkey Mind*, p.5.

15 Ageing

35 Thanissaro Bhikkhu, Upajjhatthana Sutta: Subjects for Contemplation, available at https://www.accesstoinsight.org/tipitaka/an/an05/an05.057.than.html, accessed on 18 February 2023.

36 Bhikkhuni Dhammananda, *Training the Monkey Mind*, p.23.

17 Reflections on the Ordained Life

37 'The Patimokkha recitation was done for the first time on Sunday 13th July 2003, on the eve of the rains-retreat. Symbolically speaking the recitation tends to serve as a defining activity for the existence of the monastic community.

'Venerable Dhammananda did not fail to celebrate the significance of the day. "Today is a historic day", she said at the late morning Sunday gathering of some thirty visitors and residents. "It is the first time ever a bhikkhuni sangha has recited the Patimokkha in Suwannaphum [ancient name for Thailand].' She explained that by means of the Patimokkha recitation, the *bhikkhuni borisat* (collective body of female nuns), had marked its existence."' Chamsanit, 'Reconnecting the Lost Lineage', p.261.

38 'This practice of keeping the body of a dead person for a period of time before cremation is common among Thai Buddhists in the case of respected and revered people, such as religious figures, senior members of well-to-do families and members of the royal family.' Chamsanit, 'Reconnecting the Lost Lineage', p.254.

Glossary

bhikkhu A male renunciant following the way of the Buddha; a
   fully ordained Buddhist monk.

bhikkhuni A female renunciant following the way of the Buddha; a
   Buddhist nun holding full ordination in her lineage.

Bhikkhuni Patimokkha The full set of rules of monastic discipline;
   there are 311 of them.

bodhisattva A being on the path to Buddhahood; a being intent on
   achieving enlightenment; a being with altruistic motivations;
   a Buddha-to-be who has abandoned the world but not its
   inhabitants and vows to end the suffering of others.

dalhikamma A formal confirmation or act through which monastics
   ordained elsewhere can be granted recognition by the monastic
   community of which they wish to be part. Known in the
   Theravada tradition as 'making strong'.

dasa sil mata A Sri Lankan woman who observes ten precepts and
   leads a monastic lifestyle yet has not received novice or full
   ordination.

dukkha Suffering, dissatisfaction, stress, pain, or ill-being. First of
   the four noble truths.

Kamma (Pali), Karma (Sanskrit) Simply means action; but action
   which will bear results would have to be action with intention.

kusala The wholesome, skilful, good, or meritorious actions of
   body, speech, and mind that result in favourable rebirths.
   An action characterized by this moral quality will result
   (eventually) in happiness and a favourable outcome.

mae chi Thai female renunciates who abide by five or eight
   precepts, shave their head, normally wear all white, and lead
   a Buddhist monastic lifestyle yet do not have novice or full
   ordination.

maya Deceit and self-deceit; delusion.

mahapurisa A great being, destined to become a Buddha; someone one who has reached emancipation of mind.

mahatheri An honorific term in Pali for senior bhikkhunis. The word literally means 'elder who has grown old with knowledge' and is used to distinguish those who have at least twenty years since their full ordination.

Mahayana Literally means 'the great vehicle', sometimes called the Northern school as it is predominant in China, Japan, Tibet, Korea, and Mongolia.

pavattini A female religious instructor or preceptor; a qualified nun of at least twelve years' standing who must be appointed by bhikkhu sangha, she is required to be present to ordain novice nuns and trains candidates to prepare them for full ordination.

samadhi Concentration meditation; establishing and sustaining single-pointedness of mind.

samaneri A novice nun who observes the ten precepts.

samatha Calmness, serenity, quiescence, tranquillity; peace generated through the cultivation of samadhi.

ten precepts The practices or training rules to avoid non-virtuous actions and speech observed by novice monastics. They are refraining from killing; taking that which is not given; sexual activity; false speech; intoxicants; eating after midday; dancing, singing, music, and other entertainments; adorning the body; sleeping in luxurious beds; handling money.

Theravada Literally means the words or the teaching of the elders. It is also known as the Southern school of Buddhism; it is predominant in Thailand, Sri Lanka, and Myanmar, drawing its scriptural inspiration from the Pali canon containing the earliest surviving record of the Buddha's teachings.

Tibetan Buddhism Sometimes called Vajrayana or Tantrayana. A form of Mahayana Buddhism stemming from the late stages of Indian Buddhism and including Vajrayana elements.

upasampada Full ordination as a bhikkhu or bhikkhuni.

uposatha Days of renewed dedication to Buddhist practice observed by Buddhists. This goes according to the movement of the moon on full moon, dark moon, and quarter moons.

Vajrayana A general term used to refer to tantric Buddhism; the codified practices and systems of mantras, chants, mudras, mandalas, and the visualization of deities and Buddhas.

vassa Three-month rain retreat period of concentrated study and meditation practice.

vipassana Insight meditation; clear intuitive awareness of physical and mental phenomena as they arise and disappear; seeing things as they inherently are.

Bibliography

Access to Insight, 'Glossary', available at
https://www.accesstoinsight.org/glossary.html, accessed on
13 February 2023.

Atiya Achakulwisut, 'A path less travelled', *Bangkok Post*, 17 April
2001, available at https://www.budsas.org/ebud/ebdha220a.htm,
accessed on 20 March 2023.

Atiya Achakulwisut, 'Her holiness', *Bangkok Post*, 30 May 2001,
available at https://www.budsas.org/ebud/ebdha220a.htm,
accessed on 20 March 2023.

Bhikkhu Analayo, *Bhikkhuni Ordination from Ancient India to
Contemporary Sri Lanka,* Agama Research Group, Taiwan 2023.

Bhikkhu Analayo, 'The legality of bhikkhuni ordination', *Journal of
Buddhist Ethics* 20 (2013).

Robert E. Buswell and Donald S. Lopez, *The Princeton Dictionary of
Buddhism*, Princeton University Press, Princeton 2013.

Varaporn Chamsanit, 'Reconnecting the Lost Lineage: Challenges
to Institutional Denial of Buddhist Women's Monasticism in
Thailand', PhD thesis, Australian National University, October
2006.

Bhikkhuni Dhammananda, *The Bhikkhuni Lineage*, first published
as a paper pamphlet, Nakon Pathom 2004.

Bhikkhuni Dhammananda, *Training the Monkey Mind*, Kledthai,
Bangkok 2008.

Bhikkhuni Dhammananda, *Women Strengthening Buddhism*, Thai
Tibet Center, 2010.

Sanitsuda Ekachai, 'The Dhammananda controversy', *Bangkok Post*,
22 September 2001, available at https://www.budsas.org/ebud/
ebdha220a.htm, accessed on 20 March 2023.

Koun Franz, *The Fourfold Assembly*, DharmaCrafts, 2021, available at https://dharmacrafts.com/blogs/news/the-fourfold-assembly-koun-franz, accessed on 10 June 2023.

Chatsumarn Kabilsingh, *Thai Women in Buddhism,* Parallax Press, Berkeley 1991.

Chatsumarn Kabilsingh, *Women in Buddhism Questions and Answers*, Thammasat University Press, Bangkok 1998.

Cindy Rasicot, *Finding Venerable Mother: A Daughter's Spiritual Quest to Thailand*, She Writes Press, Berkeley 2020.

Thanissaro Bhikkhu, Upajjhatthana Sutta: Subjects for Contemplation, available at https://www.accesstoinsight.org/tipitaka/an/an05/an05.057.than.html, accessed on 18 February 2023.

Yasodhara, 'Three waves of bhikkhuni sangha in Thailand', *Yasodhara* 19:4 (July–September 2003). *Yasodhara* is the title of the temple newsletter, which was published quarterly for thirty years from 1984 to 2014.

Resources

Venerable Dhammananda Bhikkhuni and Wat Songdhammakalyani Temple:

https://www.songdhammakalyani.com
Facebook: https://www.facebook.com/thaibhikkhunis2560/
YouTube: https://www.youtube.com/@DhammanandaBhikkhuni

Cindy Rasicot

https://cindyrasicot.com
Facebook: @cindy.rasicot.author
Instagram: @cindy.rasicot
Casual Buddhism on YouTube: https://www.youtube.com/@
    casualbuddhism

Illustration Credits

P.71   Venerable Dhammananda having her head shaved at novice ordination, 6 February 2001. From the personal collection of Venerable Dhammananda

P.78   Portrait of Venerable Dhammananda, 2007. Photographer: Nancy Zarider

P.79   Medicine Buddha. Photographer: Cindy Rasicot

P.81   Inscription on clay wall. Photographer: Cindy Rasicot

P.121 Venerable Dhammananda handing out rice to the local people during the pandemic. Photographer: Pathumma Ployrum

P.164 Venerable Dhammananda with her sister. Photographer: Cindy Rasicot

P.165 Cindy trying on robe. From the personal collection of Venerable Dhammananda

P.168 Picture of Cindy and Khun Richie, her English translator. From the personal collection of Venerable Dhammananda

P.171 Cindy bowing to Venerable Dhammananda. Photographer: Pimnalin Chunhawiriyakul

P.171 Venerable Dhammananda cutting the first lock of Cindy's hair. Photographer: Pimnalin Chunhawiriyakul

P.175 Cindy on alms round. Photographer: Pathumma Ployrum

P.177 Cindy after ordination. Photographer: Pimnalin Chunhawiriyakul

P.179 Venerable Dhammananda with fan. From the personal collection of Venerable Dhammananda

P.181 Young Chatsumarn Kabilsingh, age twelve. From the personal collection of Venerable Dhammananda

About the Author

Cindy Rasicot first met Venerable Dhammananda Bhikkhuni when she moved with her family to Bangkok in 2005. The encounter led to writing her memoir, *Finding Venerable Mother: A Daughter's Spiritual Quest to Thailand*, which was published in May 2020. It was on the shortlist for the 2021 Eric Hoffer Grand Prize and Sarton Award and named a 2020 CIBA Mind & Spirit Book Award finalist. Her most recent book, *This Fresh Existence: Heart Teachings from Bhikkhuni Dhammananda*, was published by Windhorse Publications in 2024.

Her writing has also appeared in *Lion's Roar*, *Elephant Journal*, and *Yasodhara*. Cindy has been featured in two anthologies: *Wandering in Paris: Luminaries and Love in the City of Light* and *A Café in Space: The Anaïs Nin Literary Journal*.

In April of 2021, Cindy and Venerable Dhammananda launched Casual Buddhism, a virtual programme inviting people from all walks of life to explore their spiritual practice with Venerable Dhammananda.

In 2014, Cindy received temporary ordination from Venerable Dhammananda and she returned to Thailand in December of 2022 to receive temporary ordination a second time.

A retired psychotherapist and writer, Cindy lives in Point Richmond, California and enjoys views of the San Francisco Bay. Learn more at cindyrasicot.com.

Index

Introductory Note

References such as '178–9' indicate (not necessarily continuous) discussion of a topic across a range of pages. Wherever possible in the case of topics with many references, these have either been divided into sub-topics or only the most significant discussions of the topic are listed. Because the entire work is about the 'Venerable Dhammananda', the use of this term (and certain others which occur constantly throughout the book) as an entry point has been restricted. Information will be found under the corresponding detailed topics.

Index

Index

WINDHORSE PUBLICATIONS

Windhorse Publications is a Buddhist charitable company based in the United Kingdom. We place great emphasis on producing books of high quality that are accessible and relevant to those interested in Buddhism at whatever level. We are the main publisher of the works of Sangharakshita, the founder of the Triratna Buddhist Order and Community. Our books draw on the whole range of the Buddhist tradition, including translations of traditional texts, commentaries, books that make links with contemporary culture and ways of life, biographies of Buddhists, and works on meditation.

As a not-for-profit enterprise, we ensure that all surplus income is invested in new books and improved production methods, to better communicate Buddhism in the twenty-first century. We welcome donations to help us continue our work – to find out more, go to windhorsepublications.com.

The Windhorse is a mythical animal that flies over the earth carrying on its back three precious jewels, bringing these invaluable gifts to all humanity: the Buddha (the 'Awakened One'), his teaching, and the community of all his followers.

Windhorse Publications
38 Newmarket Road
Cambridge CB5 8DT
info@windhorsepublications.com

Consortium Book Sales & Distribution
210 American Drive
Jackson TN 38301
USA

Windhorse Books
PO Box 574
Newtown NSW 2042
Australia

THE TRIRATNA BUDDHIST COMMUNITY

Windhorse Publications is a part of the Triratna Buddhist Community, an international movement with centres in Europe, India, North and South America, and Australasia. At these centres, members of the Triratna Buddhist Order offer classes in meditation and Buddhism. Activities of the Triratna Community also include retreat centres, residential spiritual communities, ethical Right Livelihood businesses, and the Karuna Trust, a United Kingdom fundraising charity that supports social welfare projects in the slums and villages of India.

Through these and other activities, Triratna is developing a unique approach to Buddhism, not simply as a philosophy and a set of techniques, but as a creatively directed way of life for all people living in the conditions of the modern world.

If you would like more information about Triratna please visit thebuddhistcentre.com or write to:

London Buddhist Centre
51 Roman Road
London E2 0HU
United Kingdom
contact@lbc.org.uk

Aryaloka
14 Heartwood Circle
Newmarket NH 03857
USA
info@aryaloka.org

Sydney Buddhist Centre
24 Enmore Road
Sydney NSW 2042
Australia
info@sydneybuddhistcentre.org.au

Starting on the Buddhist Path
An Invitation
Sagaraghosa

An illustrated guide to transforming your life through Buddhist practice.

The Buddha said that you can't develop wise perspective and freedom through ideas alone – you need to test the truth in your own experience. This book invites you into potentially life-changing meditations, perspectives, reflections, and practices for everyday life.

'Sagaraghosa writes with the tone of a trusted friend, sharing wisdom and perspective with a guiding grace. The book provides a safe space for readers to investigate and reflect on the delicate intricacies of developing their Buddhist practice.' – Sharon Salzberg, author of *Lovingkindness* and *Real Life*

'In Starting on the Buddhist Path, Sagaraghosa is inviting us to see and experience for ourselves the jewel that is Buddhism. This wonderful book is recommended for anyone, young or old, interested in travelling the Buddhist path to freedom.' – Vajrashura, Buddhist teacher in the Triratna Buddhist Community

'Starting on the Buddhist Path takes you by the hand – especially if you're new to Buddhism – and guides you, with great care and thoughtfulness, through Buddhist teachings and practices. As well as telling you what Buddhism says, it will help you explore why its teachings could be important for you.' – Vishvapani Blomfield, author of *Gautama Buddha: The Life and Teachings of the Awakened One*

Sagaraghosa Rosemary Tennison is an English Buddhist teacher. This is the book she wished she had when she first encountered Buddhism. She is a kind and gifted teacher, and her writing is based on 14 years of leading classes, courses, and retreats for people new to Buddhism. She was ordained into the Triratna Buddhist Order in 2005.

ISBN 978 1 915342 08 9
208 pages

Not About Being Good
A Practical Guide to Buddhist Ethics
Subhadramati

While there are numerous books on Buddhist meditation and philosophy, there are few books that are entirely devoted to the practice of Buddhist ethics. Subhadramati communicates clearly both their founding principles and the practical methods to embody them.

Buddhist ethics are not about conforming to a set of conventions, not about 'being good' in order to gain rewards. Instead, living ethically springs from the awareness that other people are no different from yourself. You can actively develop this awareness, through cultivating love, clarity, and contentment. Helping you to come into greater harmony with all that lives, this is ultimately your guidebook to a more satisfactory life.

'*In touch with the wonder of being alive, Subhadramati is a realistic and sympathetic guide to ethics in the twenty-first century.*' – Vidyamala Burch, author of *Mindfulness for Health*

'*Writing with passion, humour, and delicacy, gloriously free from moralism, her aim is to help us live a richer and fuller life.*' – Maitreyabandhu, author of *Life with Full Attention*

'*Places ethics and meditation at the heart of Buddhist practice, and shows how they work together in transforming ordinary human beings into Buddhas.*' – Professor Damien Keown, author of *The Nature of Buddhist Ethics*

1SBN 9781 909314 01 6
176 pages

Buddhism
Tools for Living Your Life
Vajragupta

In this guide for all those seeking a meaningful spiritual path, Vajragupta provides clear explanations of the main Buddhist teachings, as well as a variety of exercises designed to help readers develop or deepen their practice.

'Appealing, readable, and practical, blending accessible teachings, practices, and personal stories ... as directly relevant to modern life as it is comprehensive and rigorous.' – *Tricycle: The Buddhist Review*, 2007

'I'm very pleased that someone has finally written this book! At last, a real 'toolkit' for living a Buddhist life, his practical suggestions are hard to resist!' – Saddhanandi, Director of Adhisthana

ISBN 9781 899579 74 7
192 pages

Uncontrived Mindfulness
Ending Suffering through Attention, Curiosity and Wisdom
Vajradevi

Uncontrived Mindfulness is a fresh and comprehensive guide to awareness of how the mind shapes experience. The Buddha emphasized that happiness is found through understanding the mind rather than getting caught up in sense experience. This simple yet radical shift is key to a relaxed and uncontrived way of practising. Freedom comes from uniting right view and mindfulness.

A deep dive into the practice of exploring our experience as it happens, Vajradevi's emphasis is on cultivating wisdom, using the tools of attention, curiosity, and discernment to recognize and see through the delusion that is causing our suffering.

Vajradevi is a warm and insightful guide to this exploration, drawing on her intensive and wide-ranging-practice of satipaṭṭhāna meditation. The clear explanations and instructions are amplified by Vajradevi's personal accounts, charting her uncompromising voyage into self-discovery. Guided meditations are included.

'Vajradevi is a practitioner who shares her own experience of practising mindfulness simply and clearly. She makes traditional concepts accessible because she knows them from the inside, and this book is full of stories of how Vajradevi has learned to be mindful of her own life.' – Vishvapani Blomfield, author of *Gautama Buddha: The Life and Teachings of the Awakened One*

'A wonderful book, written with that independence of mind characteristic of deep practitioners.' – Kamalashila, meditation teacher and author of *Buddhist Meditation: Tranquillity, Imagination & Insight*

'Vajradevi gives relevant and real examples which show us that dedicating ourselves to mindfulness does not mean being cut off from life. I loved reading the stories she weaves in to explain her journey in mindfulness and the thoughtful connections she makes with common doubts or questions about the practice, the journey, and its effects.' – Ma Thet, translator for Sayadaw U Tejaniya

Vajradevi grew up on the Isle of Wight and met the Dharma at the age of 23. She was ordained into the Triratna Buddhist Order in 1995. For the past twenty years she has explored and taught meditation based on the *Satipaṭṭhāna Sutta*, the Buddha's primary teaching on mindfulness. She spent a year in Myanmar on retreat with Sayadaw U Tejaniya, and leads retreats in the UK and Europe that teach mindfulness as a path to wisdom.

ISBN 978-1-911407-61-4
248 pages

The Subtle Art of Caring
A Guide to Sustaining Compassion
River Wolton

An inspired guide to sustaining compassion for carers and activists.

The Buddha taught the 'divine abodes' of loving kindness, compassion, empathetic joy, and equanimity, which are guides to embodiment and relaxing the sense of self. Poet, writer, activist, mentor and Buddhist teacher River Wolton gives new life to these teachings as resources for a life in which compassion and justice for self and other are mutually sustaining. This book is beautifully illustrated and with exercises, meditations, and reflections.

'Using as a template the five qualities of pausing, befriending, enjoying, caring, and letting be, [River Wolton] shows the way to a profoundly beneficial life for ourselves and others.' – Martine Batchelor

'If you wish to explore how to take Buddhism off the meditation cushion and into the world, read this book.' – Dene Donalds

'River reveals the powerful ways we can contribute to the end of distress through transforming our own hearts.' – Christina Feldman

'River Wolton leads us with unfailing insight to that difficult place where individual Buddhist practice meets the urgent global issues of our time.... An important read for the Anthropocene age.' – Akasharaja

'This book is a tonic for our times. Read and respair (rebuild hope and recover from despair)!' – Prof. Rebecca Crane

'River Wolton...steer[s] us through the labyrinth of caring in a seemingly uncaring world.' – Dharmacharini Anagarika Parami

'[River]...stories how mindful awareness can transmute the inner and outer crises of distress and disconnection. A toolkit of creative explorations, rituals, and reflections....' – Jennifer Radloff

River Wolton trained as a social worker and psychotherapist. She leads writing workshops in schools and community projects, and is a peace and LGBTQI+ activist. Co-founder of Sheffield Insight Meditation, she teaches Buddhist retreats at Gaia House, UK. She was the Poet Laureate for Derbyshire and has published three volumes of poetry.

Emma Burleigh is an artist, illustrator, comics creator, and teacher. She is the author of two art course books, *Soul Color* and *Earh Color*, which are designed to nurture mindfulness, creativity, and nature connectedness.

ISBN 978 1 915342 21 8
224 pages

Mindfulness of Breathing
A Practice Guide and Translations
Bhikkhu Anālayo

Buddhist scholar and teacher Bhikkhu Anālayo explores the practice of mindfulness of breathing in the sixteen steps of the *Ānāpānasati Sutta*. This is an authoritative, practice-orientated elucidation of a foundational Buddhist text, useful to meditators whatever their tradition or background.

In the first six chapters Anālayo presents practical instructions comparable to his *Satipaṭṭhāna Meditation: A Practice Guide*. The remaining chapters contain his translations of extracts from the early Chinese canon. With his accompanying commentary, these help the practitioner appreciate the early Buddhist perspective on the breath and the practice of mindfulness of breathing.

Anālayo presents his understanding of these early teachings, arising from his own meditation practice and teaching experience. His aim is to inspire all practitioners to use what he has found helpful to build their own practice and become self-reliant.

'In this book Bhikkhu Anālayo explores the seminal topic of ānāpānasati *with characteristic thoroughness, openness, and skilful reference to the textual tradition behind this practice. Through linking the central theme to topics such as walking meditation and the aggregates, he broadens its relevance to a wide range of Dhamma-cultivation. Here then is a valuable resource for us to dip into, or to steadily work through, to gain access to this liberating practice.'* – Ajahn Sucitto

'Bhikkhu Anālayo's genius is, in part, to analyse the terse, sometimes obscure language of the Buddha's discourses and reveal them as fresh, practical guidance for contemporary meditators. Here the author takes up the discourse on mindfulness of breathing to lead us phrase by phrase into clear, precise instructions to calm the mind and realize the Buddha's deepest insights. The most complete and in-depth guide available for this classic meditation.' – Guy Armstrong, author of *Emptiness: A Practical Guide for Meditators*

'Practical, inspiring, thought provoking! This book achieves two great aims. First it offers meditators a clear practice sequence that is easy to apply. And second, it presents new translations and thoughtful analysis based on a comparative study of early Buddhist texts. This practical and thoughtful interpretation of the Buddha's sixteen steps will surely inspire readers to re-discover the joyful and liberating potential of mindfulness with breathing.' – Shaila Catherine, author of *Focused and Fearless: A Meditator's Guide to States of Deep Joy, Calm, and Clarity*

ISBN 978 1 911407 44 7
320 pages

Printed in the USA
CPSIA information can be obtained
at www.ICGtesting.com
JSHW011441010424
60353JS00012B/174

9 781915 342317